ICAEW
Law

First edition 2007, Fourteenth edition 2020

ISBN 978 1 5097 3413 9

British Library Cataloguing-in-Publication Data
A catalogue record for this book is available from the
British Library

Published by

BPP Learning Media Ltd
BPP House, Aldine Place
142–144 Uxbridge Road,
London W12 8AA

www.bpp.com/learningmedia

Printed in the United Kingdom

Your learning materials, published by BPP Learning
Media Ltd, are printed on paper obtained from traceable,
sustainable sources.

Welcome to BPP Learning Media's **Passcards** for ICAEW **Law**.

- They **save you time**. Important topics are summarised for you.

- They incorporate **diagrams** to kick start your memory.

- They follow the overall **structure** of the ICAEW Workbook, but BPP Learning Media's ICAEW **Passcards** are not just a condensed book. Each card has been separately designed for clear presentation. Topics are self-contained and can be grasped visually.

- ICAEW **Passcards** are **just the right size** for pockets, briefcases and bags.

- ICAEW **Passcards focus on the exams** you will be facing.

Run through the **Passcards** as often as you can during your final revision period. The day before the exam, try to go through the **Passcards** again! You will then be well on your way to passing your exams.

Good luck!

Contents

1: Contract formation

Topic List

Validity of a contract

Offer and acceptance

Intention to create legal relations

Consideration

Terms of a contract

Privity of contract

This chapter explains the essential characteristics of a valid and legally binding contract. It also examines the enforceable terms of a contract and describes the doctrine of privity of contract, concerned with who may enforce a contract.

A sound grasp of the fundamental rules of contract law is essential.

Contract

A valid contract is a legally binding agreement, supported by valid consideration, between two parties who intend to create legal relations

Three essential elements for a valid contract

- Agreement (usually offer and acceptance)
- Intention to create legal relations
- Consideration

Even if these three elements are present, the contract may still be void, voidable or unenforcable

Freedom of contract

The principle that the law will not generally interfere with the parties' ability to contract on whatever terms they wish

Standard form contract

One prepared by the dominant party on a take-it-or-leave-it basis

However, the law **may** intervene especially where there is unequal bargaining power, eg:

- **Sale of Goods Act**, to imply conditions as to the fitness of goods
- **Consumer Credit Act**, to protect the consumer taking credit
- **Unfair Contract Terms Act**, to prevent the dominant party from relying on a clause excluding or limiting liability unfairly

A contract may be:

Void

Where it is

- Illegal
- Offends public policy

Which means that

- Not a contract at all
- Not binding on either party
- Property usually recoverable, even from third party

Voidable

Where there is

- Duress
- Undue influence
- Misrepresentation

Which means that

- One party may set it aside
- Property usually irrecoverable from third party

Unenforceable

Where it is

- Not in the correct form required by law

Which means that

- Performance by the defaulting party cannot be compelled, ie, enforced in a court of law

General rule

A contract may be in any form:

- Oral
- Written
- Inferred from conduct

Exceptions

- Agreement for transfer of land must be in writing
- Certain consumer credit agreements must be in writing
- Guarantee must be evidenced in writing and acknowledged by a guarantor

1: Contract formation

Offer

An **offer** is a definite promise to be bound on specific terms. It is made by an **offeror** to an **offeree**.

It may be made to the world at large or to a specific person or persons

General rule: Offer + Acceptance = Agreement

However, note (a) 'Acceptance' in ignorance of the offer will not amount to agreement (nb reward cases)

(b) Agreement may be deduced from circumstances without need for offer and acceptance (eg, members being bound by a club's rules)

Invitation to treat

An invitation to treat is an indication that a person is ready to receive offers

An offer is **not**

- A vague statement, unless it can be rendered certain by reference to previous dealings or custom
- A statement of intention
- An invitation to treat

None of these is capable of acceptance to form a binding contract

Invitations to treat – examples

- Goods exhibited for sale in shop window
- Advertisements
- Circulation of price list

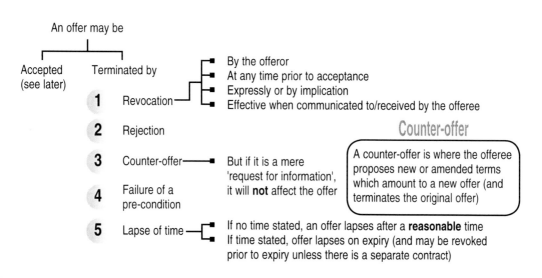

An offer may be

Accepted (see later)

Terminated by

1 Revocation
- By the offeror
- At any time prior to acceptance
- Expressly or by implication
- Effective when communicated to/received by the offeree

2 Rejection

3 Counter-offer ——— But if it is a mere 'request for information', it will **not** affect the offer

Counter-offer

A counter-offer is where the offeree proposes new or amended terms which amount to a new offer (and terminates the original offer)

4 Failure of a pre-condition

5 Lapse of time
- If no time stated, an offer lapses after a **reasonable** time
- If time stated, offer lapses on expiry (and may be revoked prior to expiry unless there is a separate contract)

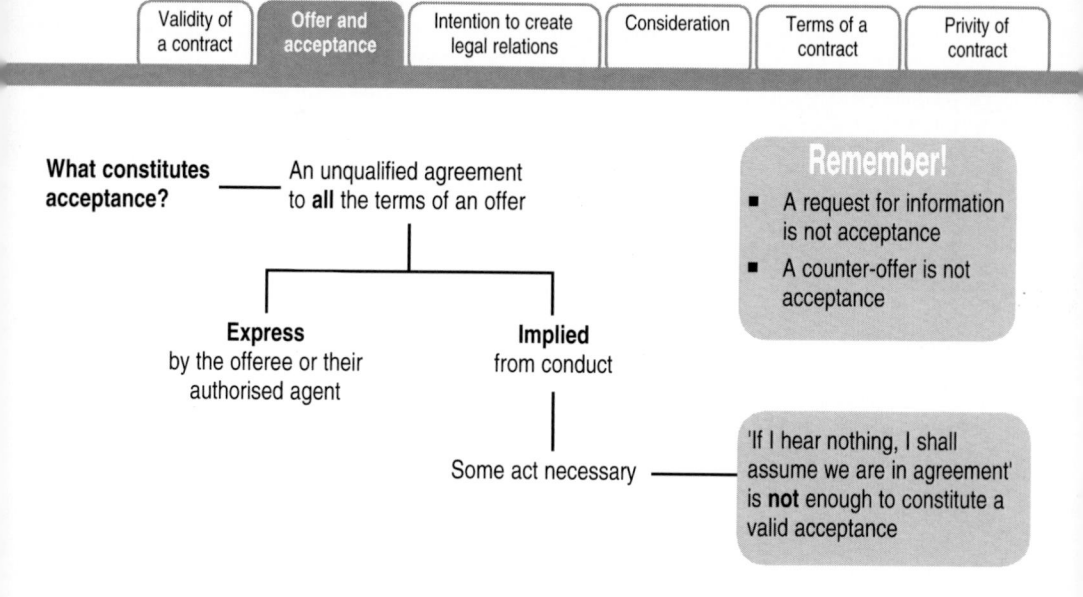

What constitutes acceptance? — An unqualified agreement to **all** the terms of an offer

Express
by the offeree or their authorised agent

Implied
from conduct

Some act necessary

Remember!
- A request for information is not acceptance
- A counter-offer is not acceptance

'If I hear nothing, I shall assume we are in agreement' is **not** enough to constitute a valid acceptance

When is acceptance effective? ____ When it is **communicated** ____ **UNLESS** ____ (a) The postal rule applies, or
to the offeror

(b) The offeror waives the need for communication, either expressly or by implication

The postal rule

Prescribed method of communication

- Offeree should use prescribed method
- Or no less expeditious alternative method

No prescribed method of communication

- Offeree may use any reasonable method

Provided

(1) Post is in the contemplation of the parties (Note: Acceptance 'by notice in writing' means the rule will **not** apply)

(2) The acceptance is not delayed or lost due to offeree's negligence

Then acceptance is effective as soon as it is posted

Intention to create legal relations $=$ Second essential element for valid contract

In the absence of clear intention, apply **rebuttable presumption**

- **Social**, **domestic** or **family** arrangements — ☒ No intention to create legal relations

- **Commercial** arrangement — ☑ Intention to create legal relations

Evidence of rebuttal

- Parties are husband and wife living apart
- Agreement relates to property

'Ex gratia'

Not enough to rebut presumption

'Subject to contract'

Words provide a strong indication that the parties do **not** intend to create legal relations

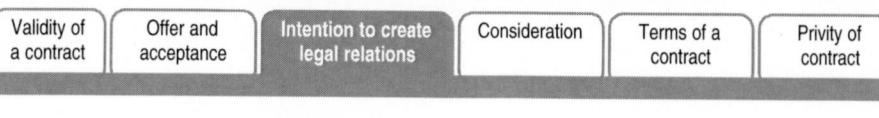

Consideration = Third essential element in a valid contract

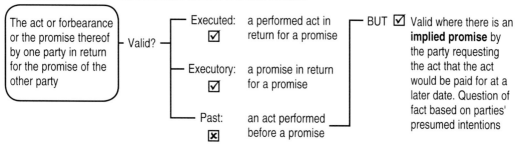

The act or forbearance or the promise thereof by one party in return for the promise of the other party — Valid?

— Executed: a performed act in return for a promise ☑

— Executory: a promise in return for a promise ☑

— Past: an act performed before a promise ☒

BUT ☑ Valid where there is an **implied promise** by the party requesting the act that the act would be paid for at a later date. Question of fact based on parties' presumed intentions

Rules **1** **Consideration need not be adequate** → the law will not weigh up the comparative values of the promises or acts exchanged

2 **Consideration must be sufficient** → ie, it must have some identifiable value (see next)

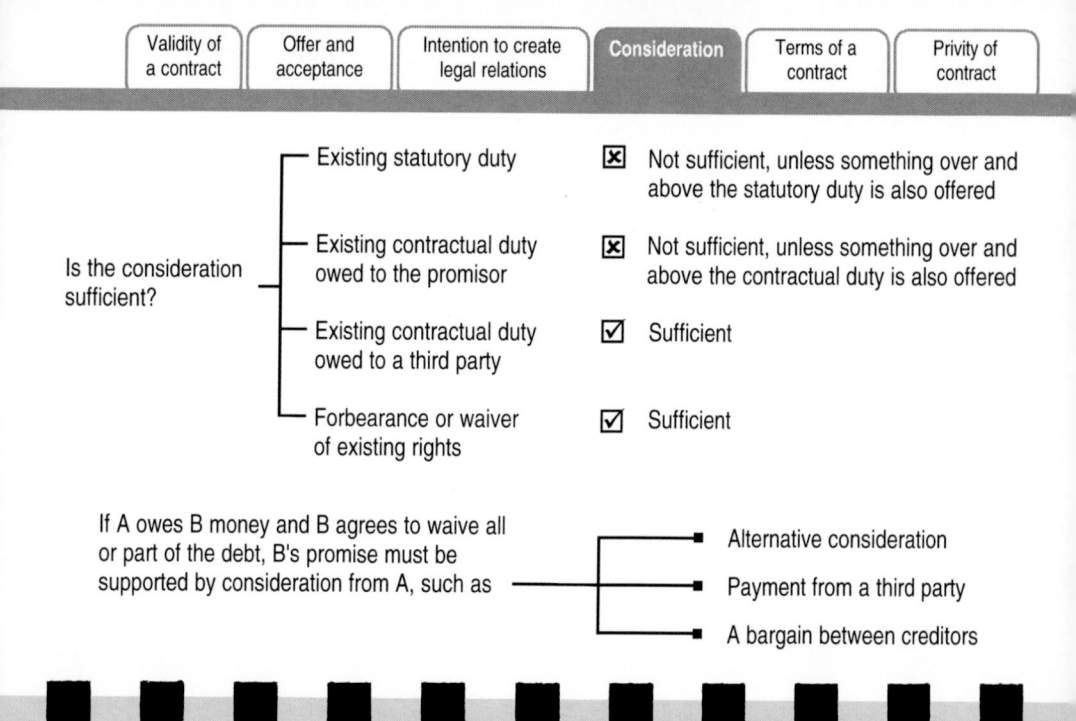

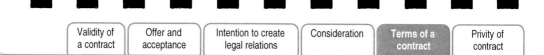

Oral contract ─────────■ Question of fact

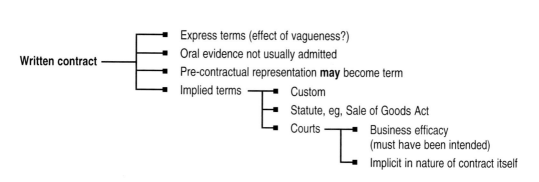

Written contract ───┬──■ Express terms (effect of vagueness?)
                    ├──■ Oral evidence not usually admitted
                    ├──■ Pre-contractual representation **may** become term
                    └──■ Implied terms ──┬──■ Custom
                                     ├──■ Statute, eg, Sale of Goods Act
                                     └──■ Courts ──┬──■ Business efficacy (must have been intended)
                                                       └──■ Implicit in nature of contract itself

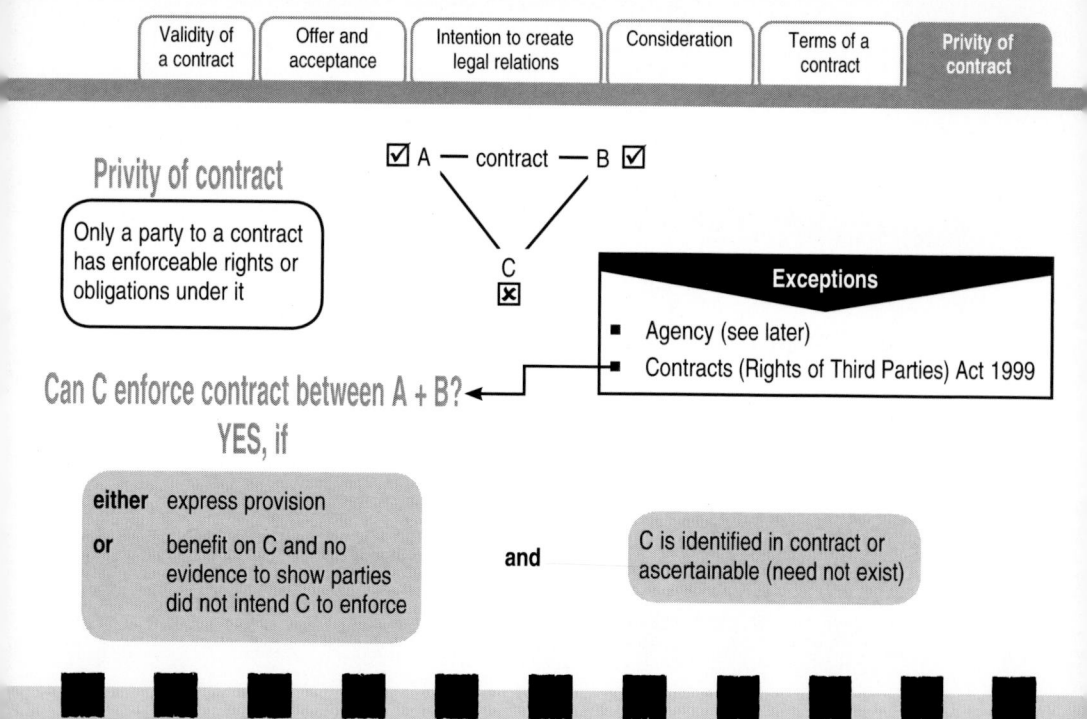

Privity of contract

Only a party to a contract has enforceable rights or obligations under it

A ─ contract ─ B ☑ ☑

C ☒

Exceptions

- Agency (see later)
- Contracts (Rights of Third Parties) Act 1999

Can C enforce contract between A + B?
YES, if

either express provision

or benefit on C and no evidence to show parties did not intend C to enforce

and

C is identified in contract or ascertainable (need not exist)

2: Termination of contract

Chapter 2 looks at how a contract is discharged or terminated by performance, frustration or breach.

It describes the various remedies available in the event of a breach of contract and considers whether an exclusion clause can be relied upon to exclude or restrict legal liability.

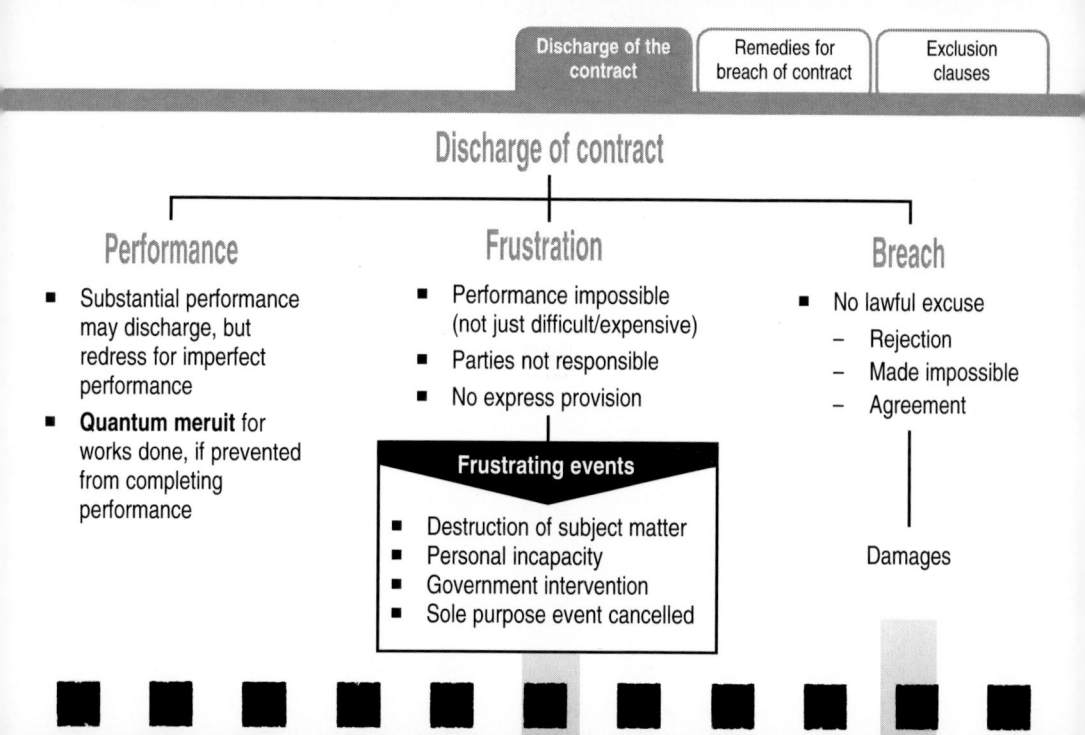

Discharge of contract

Performance

- Substantial performance may discharge, but redress for imperfect performance
- **Quantum meruit** for works done, if prevented from completing performance

Frustration

- Performance impossible (not just difficult/expensive)
- Parties not responsible
- No express provision

Frustrating events

- Destruction of subject matter
- Personal incapacity
- Government intervention
- Sole purpose event cancelled

Breach

- No lawful excuse
  - Rejection
  - Made impossible
  - Agreement

Damages

- Recover monies paid
- Sums due no longer payable
- Set off/recover expenses
- Valuable benefit

Very serious breach?
- Fundamental term
- Anticipatory breach
→ ■ Elect to

Affirm   Treat as terminated
- Notify party
- Discharge from future performance
- Reclaim money paid/ refuse to pay if defective performance

Severable contract

Contract can effectively be divided into smaller contracts

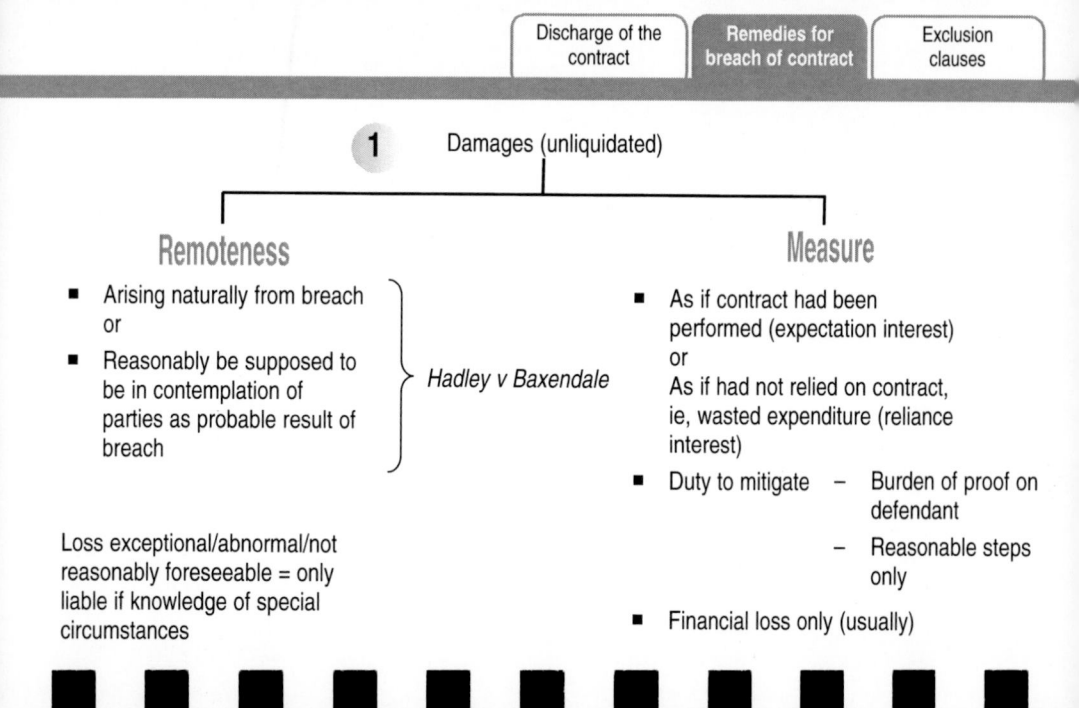

1 Damages (unliquidated)

Remoteness

- Arising naturally from breach
  or
- Reasonably be supposed to be in contemplation of parties as probable result of breach

} *Hadley v Baxendale*

Loss exceptional/abnormal/not reasonably foreseeable = only liable if knowledge of special circumstances

Measure

- As if contract had been performed (expectation interest)
  or
  As if had not relied on contract, ie, wasted expenditure (reliance interest)
- Duty to mitigate — Burden of proof on defendant
  — Reasonable steps only
- Financial loss only (usually)

2   Liquidated damages: In proportion to protect the legitimate
interest of the innocent party   ☑

Penal in nature   ☒ — Penalty clause void

3   Specific performance
- Equitable remedy
- Only where damages inadequate
- Not if personal or supervision required

4   Injunction
- Mandatory (rare)
- Prohibitory
- Asset-freezing

Exclusion clause

Clause purporting to exclude or restrict liability for breach of contract or negligence

☑ Properly incorporated
- At or before contract
- Integral part of contract

- Signed: binding unless misleading explanation
- Unsigned: show party made aware of it

☑ Ambiguity interpreted against person relying on it

UCTA 1977 (B2B contracts)

The main provisions of UCTA can be summarised as follows:

Attempts to exclude or restrict liability for death or personal injury arising from negligence are void.

Attempts to restrict liability for other loss or damage arising from negligence are void unless they can be shown to be reasonable.

Clauses that attempt to exclude or limit liability for breach of the undertakings as to title of the seller or owner, implied by the Sale of Goods Act 1979, are void.

Consumer Rights Act 2015 (B2C contracts)

Terms will only be binding on the consumer if they are 'fair'. However, the consumer may still rely on a term which is deemed 'unfair'.

Terms must be set out in plain, intelligible language and any relevant terms must be prominent.

3: Agency

This chapter describes how an agency relationship comes into existence and the main rights and duties of the agent and principal. It also explains the nature of an agent's authority and how the liability of the respective parties is determined.

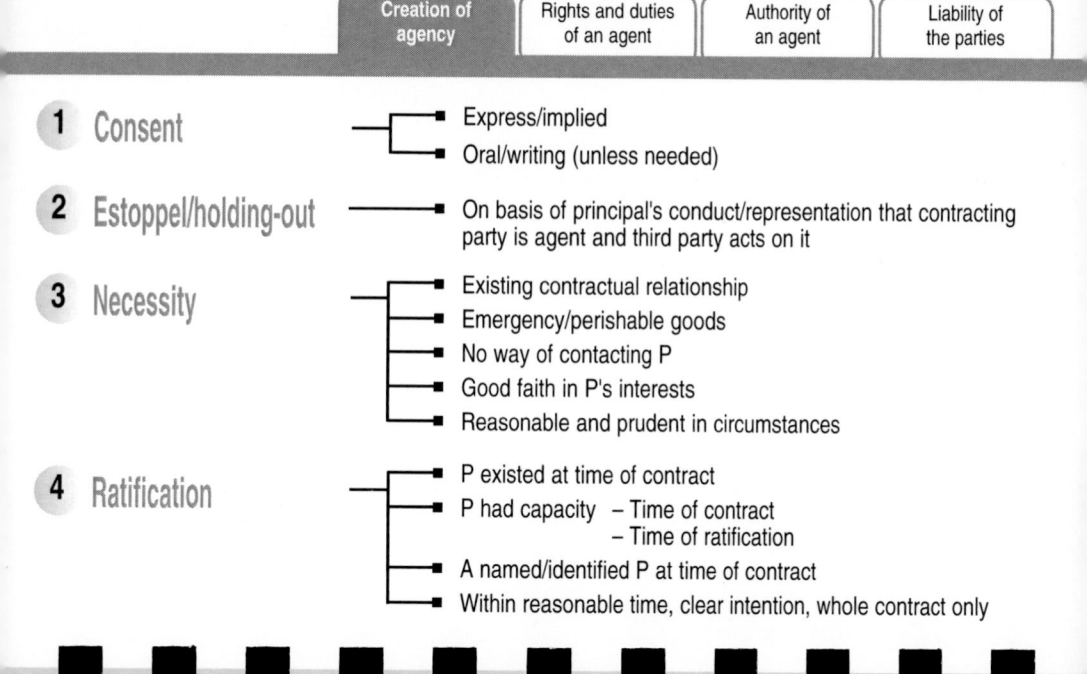

Creation of agency	Rights and duties of an agent	Authority of an agent	Liability of the parties

1 Consent
- Express/implied
- Oral/writing (unless needed)

2 Estoppel/holding-out
- On basis of principal's conduct/representation that contracting party is agent and third party acts on it

3 Necessity
- Existing contractual relationship
- Emergency/perishable goods
- No way of contacting P
- Good faith in P's interests
- Reasonable and prudent in circumstances

4 Ratification
- P existed at time of contract
- P had capacity – Time of contract
  – Time of ratification
- A named/identified P at time of contract
- Within reasonable time, clear intention, whole contract only

Duties implied by law

Agent	Principal
■ Accountability – information/monies	■ Indemnity
■ Avoid conflict	■ Remuneration
■ Performance – not if illegal	■ Lien
■ Obedience to lawful and reasonable instructions	
■ Skill and care	
■ Not to delegate	
■ Confidentiality	

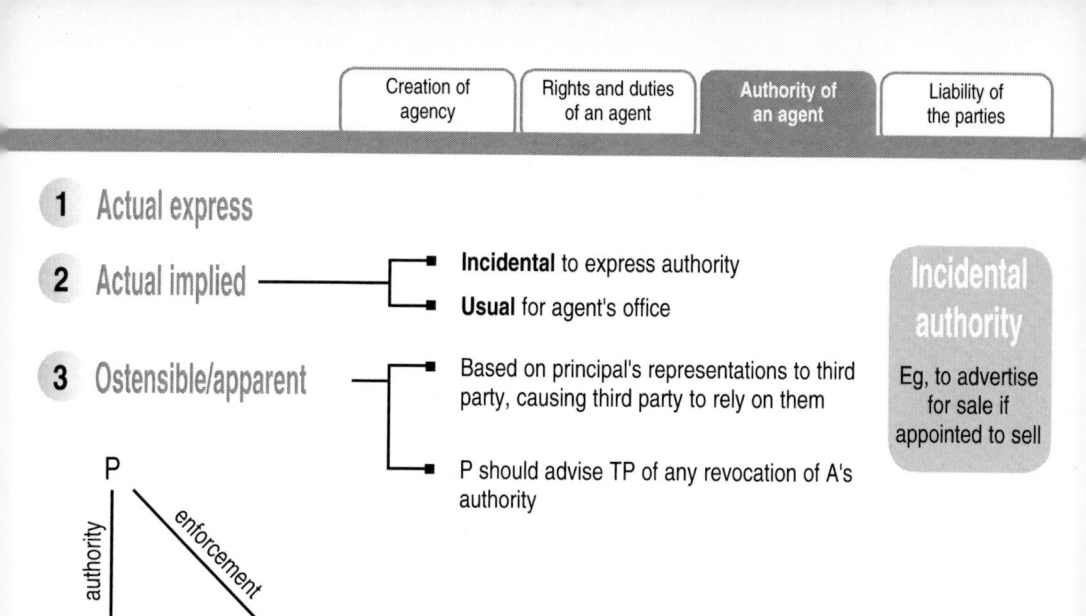

1 Actual express

2 Actual implied
- **Incidental** to express authority
- **Usual** for agent's office

3 Ostensible/apparent
- Based on principal's representations to third party, causing third party to rely on them
- P should advise TP of any revocation of A's authority

Incidental authority

Eg, to advertise for sale if appointed to sell

P

A ———— TP

authority

enforcement

contract

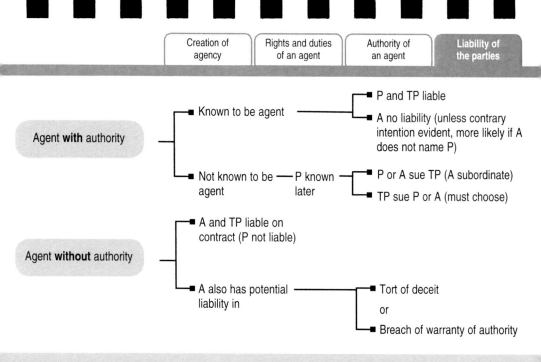

Agent with authority

- Known to be agent
  - P and TP liable
  - A no liability (unless contrary intention evident, more likely if A does not name P)
- Not known to be agent — P known later
  - P or A sue TP (A subordinate)
  - TP sue P or A (must choose)

Agent without authority

- A and TP liable on contract (P not liable)
- A also has potential liability in
  - Tort of deceit
  - or
  - Breach of warranty of authority

Notes

4: Negligence

Chapter 4 examines the concept of tort and negligence in particular. The question of whether a duty of care arises in cases where professional advice is given is especially relevant. The chapter sets out the three essential elements of a successful claim for negligence and describes the principal defences available and the main remedy of damages. It also addresses the question of vicarious liability, where a tort is committed by an employee or other agent.

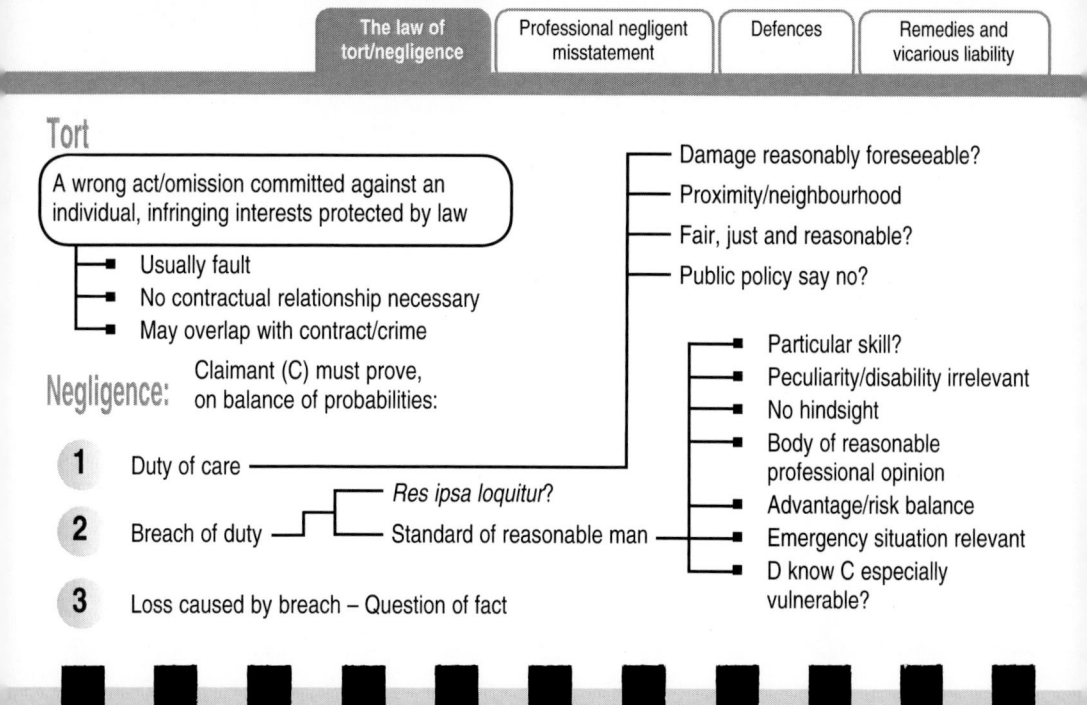

Tort

A wrong act/omission committed against an individual, infringing interests protected by law

- Usually fault
- No contractual relationship necessary
- May overlap with contract/crime

Negligence: Claimant (C) must prove, on balance of probabilities:

1 Duty of care
- Damage reasonably foreseeable?
- Proximity/neighbourhood
- Fair, just and reasonable?
- Public policy say no?

2 Breach of duty
- *Res ipsa loquitur?*
- Standard of reasonable man
  - Particular skill?
  - Peculiarity/disability irrelevant
  - No hindsight
  - Body of reasonable professional opinion
  - Advantage/risk balance
  - Emergency situation relevant
  - D know C especially vulnerable?

3 Loss caused by breach – Question of fact

Professional negligence

- Economic loss
- No liability outside professional context
- Usually question of whether duty of care exists

> **It is not unreasonable for auditors to include a disclaimer stating that they do not accept responsibility to anyone other than the addressees of the audit report.**

- Not (generally) to existing or potential investors considering their investments (Caparo)
- Not to unknown takeover bidder
- Not where statement prepared for general circulation

Alert! Causation still needs to be shown – JEB case: takeover for reason other than accounts

Factors

- Relationship between parties
- Knowledge of parties
- Purpose of advice
- Extent of C's reliance
- Intended/known that C would rely?
- Representations made?
- Assumption of responsibility?
- Fair and equitable?
- Size of class to which C belongs

Defences to negligence

1   Contributory negligence   ———   Reduce damages by % representing degree of fault (Law Reform (CN) Act 1945)

2   Volenti non fit injuria   ———   Knowledge of/consent to risk **not** sufficient

———   Effectively agreement to exempt D from duty of care, ie, accept no legal redress

———   Volenti will not override UCTA

3   Exclusion clause   ———   UCTA ———   Death or personal injury: VOID

———   Other damage: reasonableness test

Liability for audited accounts

- Attempt to exclude liability **void** unless in **liability limitation agreement** under CA 2006
- Indemnity for costs in defending proceedings is permitted

| The law of tort/negligence | Professional negligent misstatement | Defences | **Remedies and vicarious liability** |

Remedies

1 Injunction (rare)

2 Damages (compensatory lump sum)

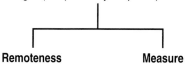

Remoteness

- **Type** of damage must be reasonably foreseeable
- Extent/manner of damage does **not** have to be reasonably foreseeable
- If damage intentional, never too remote

Measure

- As if tortious act not committed and loss not suffered

Vicarious liability

In addition to liability of tortfeasor

Of employer

- For employee's torts **not** independent contractor's
- Acting in course of employment closely connected to employment (*Lister's* case)

Of principal

- For torts of agent acting with authority
- In carrying out tasks for which appointed

Notes

5: Companies: the consequences of incorporation

Topic List

Characteristics of a company

Types of company

Formation of a company

A company's name

Articles of association

Administrative consequences of incorporation

Accounts and audit requirements

This chapter looks at the conceptual, practical and administrative consequences of a business being incorporated as a registered company. It describes the different types of company and explains how a company is formed. It also describes the articles of association, a company's principal constitutional document, and lists the various administrative steps that need to be taken by a business once incorporated.

Salomon v Salomon 1897 = landmark case that established the **separate legal personality** of a company

Legal person(s)

Registered company

- Company assets and liabilities belong to the company
- Company has insurable interest
- Company continues in existence despite any membership changes
- Company may have liability in contract, tort and crime
- Company is liable without limit for its debts (whether limited or unlimited company)

Veil of incorporation drawn between company/its members

The veil may be lifted

Members

- Liability of the members (not the company) may be limited
- Relevant where company wound up and its assets are insufficient to meet its liabilities

Members' liability limited to

Limited by shares
- Amount of nominal value outstanding plus
- Amount of premium outstanding (if original shareholder)

Limited by guarantee
- Amount guaranteed to pay on winding up

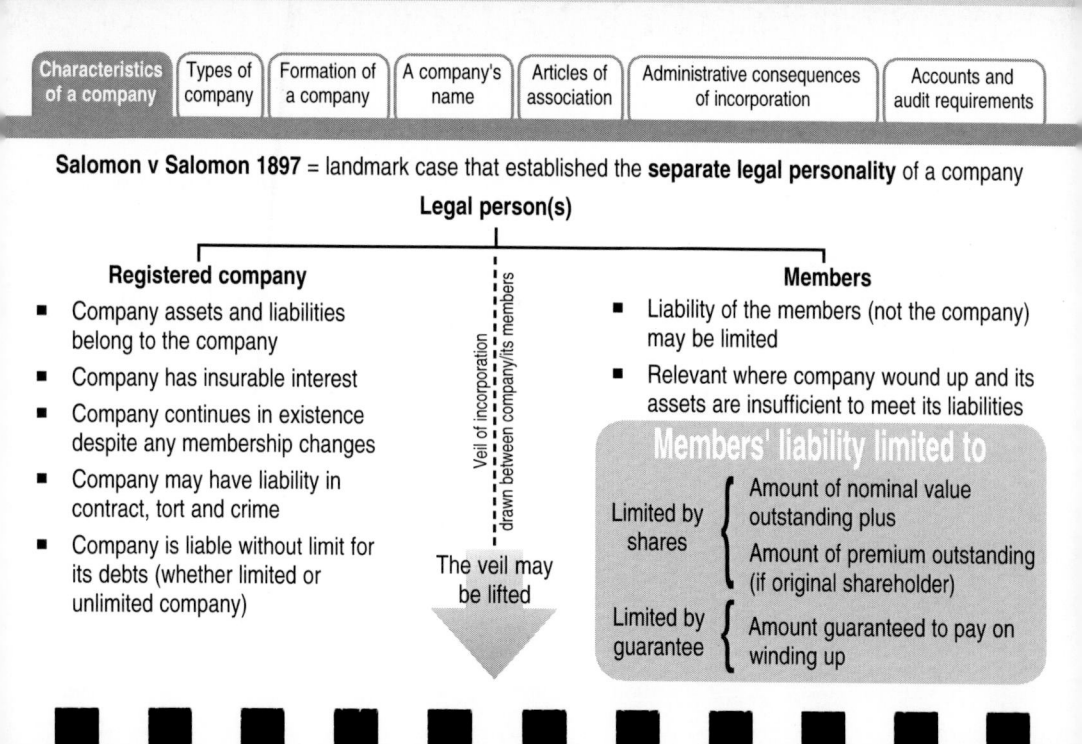

Lifting of the veil

By the courts

1 Where **subsidiary effectively acting as agent** for holding company

> **Alert!** There is no general principle that group companies will be identified as a single entity, even if a subsidiary becomes insolvent despite asset-wealth of holding company

2 To establish true **national identity** based on members' domicile, rather than registered office, to expose sham or illegality

3 To allow just and equitable winding up in **quasi-partnership company**, where director excluded from management

4 To **expose sham**, eg, company set up purely to avoid legal obligation

By statute

■ To impose liability on directors eg,

1 **Disqualified director** continuing to participate in management

   ■ Liable with company for company's debts

2 **Fraudulent or wrongful trading**

   ■ Liable to contribute to company's debts

3 Where company trades without **trading certificate**

   ■ Liable for third party losses

5: Companies: the consequences of incorporation

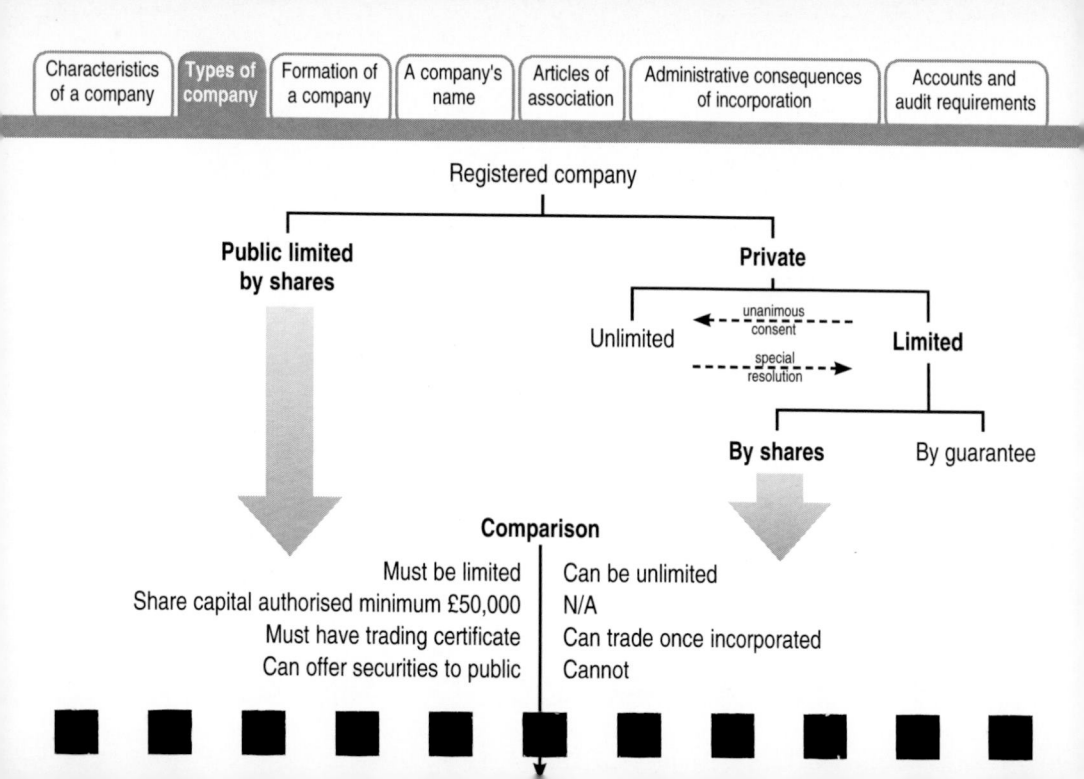

Registered company

Public limited by shares

Private

unanimous consent ←

Unlimited

special resolution →

Limited

By shares   By guarantee

Comparison

Must be limited	Can be unlimited
Share capital authorised minimum £50,000	N/A
Must have trading certificate	Can trade once incorporated
Can offer securities to public	Cannot

'Public limited company' or 'plc'	'Limited' or 'Ltd'
Approval for loans	N/A
Minimum two directors	Minimum one
Must have company secretary	N/A
Must hold AGM	N/A
Accounts and reports before general meeting	N/A
File within six months	File within nine months
Appoint auditors annually	Deemed re-appointed
Pre-emption rights compulsory	May be excluded
Shares 1/4 paid up	N/A
Valuations for non-cash consideration	N/A
Reduction of capital: special resolution and court order	No court order
N/A	Can pass written resolutions
N/A	Small and medium sized company advantages
N/A	Power to redeem/purchase shares out of capital

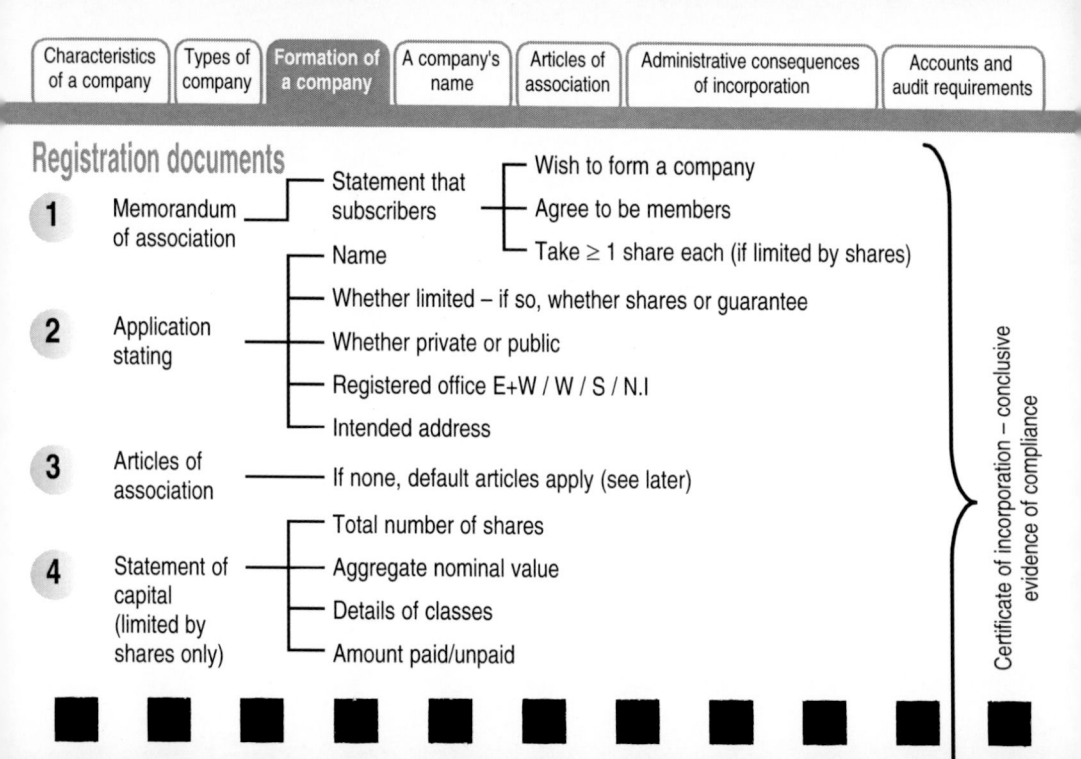

Registration documents

1 Memorandum of association
— Statement that subscribers
  — Wish to form a company
  — Agree to be members
  — Take ≥ 1 share each (if limited by shares)

2 Application stating
— Name
— Whether limited – if so, whether shares or guarantee
— Whether private or public
— Registered office E+W / W / S / N.I
— Intended address

3 Articles of association
— If none, default articles apply (see later)

4 Statement of capital (limited by shares only)
— Total number of shares
— Aggregate nominal value
— Details of classes
— Amount paid/unpaid

Certificate of incorporation – conclusive evidence of compliance

5	Statement of proposed officers	— Particulars and consent of	┌ Directors
			└ Company secretary (if applicable)

6 Statement of compliance
(the requirements of the Companies Act have been complied with)

7 Statement of guarantee

8 Application for trading certificate (public only) ┌ Share capital ≥ authorised minimum
└ Statement of compliance

Alternative: 'off-the-shelf company'

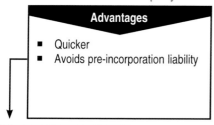

Advantages	Disadvantages
■ Quicker ■ Avoids pre-incorporation liability	Changes may be needed to ■ Name ■ Directors/company secretary ■ Subscribers ■ Articles

5: Companies: the consequences of incorporation

Promoter

Someone who makes business preparations for company (but not solicitor/accountant acting in normal professional capacity in business formation)

Owes duties
- Reasonable care and skill
- Fiduciary duty to disclose personal interest and account for monies received
  - Public: listing particulars/prospectus
  - Private: board of directors

Personal liability on pre-incorporation contracts
- Company cannot ratify (not exist when made)
- Company not bound by it (even if derived benefit)
- Company cannot enforce it (unless C(R of TP)A applies)

No right to expenses/indemnity, must make express provision

Alert! C(R of TP) Act 1999 provides that original parties remain liable, so giving company rights not sufficient in itself

Ways to avoid promoter's liability

- Not make contract until company formed
- Agree draft only, expressly on basis that company will enter into the contract with the other party, once incorporated
- Use off-the-shelf company
- Novation of contract by company and third party consent to promoter's release

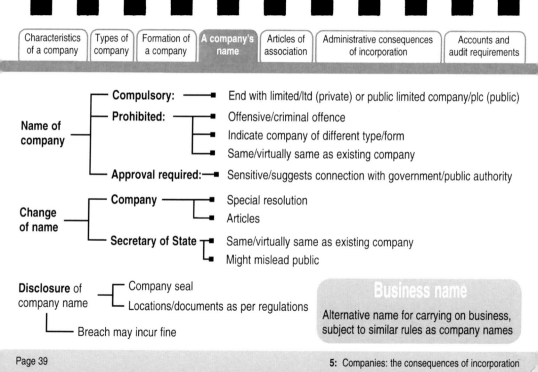

Name of company
- **Compulsory:** — End with limited/ltd (private) or public limited company/plc (public)
- **Prohibited:**
  - Offensive/criminal offence
  - Indicate company of different type/form
  - Same/virtually same as existing company
- **Approval required:** — Sensitive/suggests connection with government/public authority

Change of name
- **Company**
  - Special resolution
  - Articles
- **Secretary of State**
  - Same/virtually same as existing company
  - Might mislead public

Disclosure of company name
- Company seal
- Locations/documents as per regulations
- Breach may incur fine

Business name

Alternative name for carrying on business, subject to similar rules as company names

Articles

Regulations governing the internal management of a company's affairs; rights of shareholders and powers and duties of directors

Model Articles

Prescribed by Secretary of State in respect of different types of companies – apply in default, where none submitted or where articles insufficient

Conflict: In the event of conflict between articles and CA'06, the Act will prevail

Constitution

A company's articles, special resolutions and other relevant resolutions and agreements

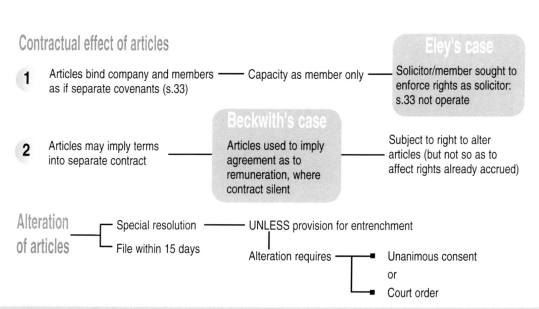

Contractual effect of articles

1 Articles bind company and members as if separate covenants (s.33) —— Capacity as member only

Eley's case

Solicitor/member sought to enforce rights as solicitor: s.33 not operate

2 Articles may imply terms into separate contract ——

Beckwith's case

Articles used to imply agreement as to remuneration, where contract silent

Subject to right to alter articles (but not so as to affect rights already accrued)

Alteration of articles

- Special resolution —— UNLESS provision for entrenchment
- File within 15 days

Alteration requires ——
- Unanimous consent

or

- Court order

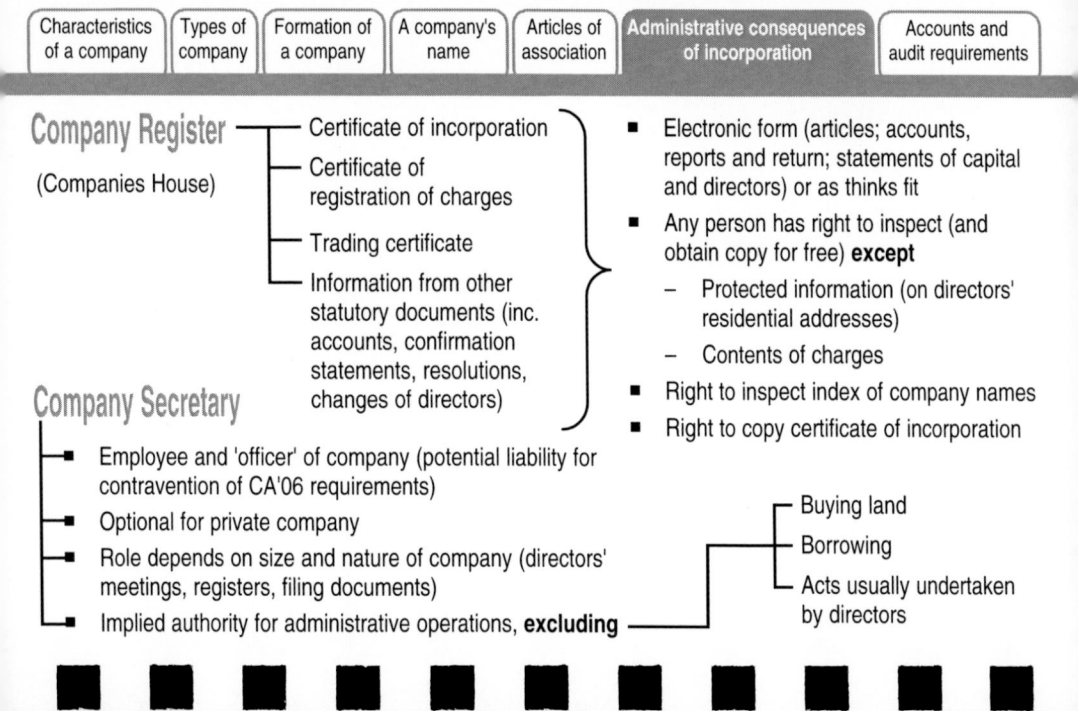

Company Register

(Companies House)

- Certificate of incorporation
- Certificate of registration of charges
- Trading certificate
- Information from other statutory documents (inc. accounts, confirmation statements, resolutions, changes of directors)

- Electronic form (articles; accounts, reports and return; statements of capital and directors) or as thinks fit
- Any person has right to inspect (and obtain copy for free) **except**
  - Protected information (on directors' residential addresses)
  - Contents of charges
- Right to inspect index of company names
- Right to copy certificate of incorporation

Company Secretary

- Employee and 'officer' of company (potential liability for contravention of CA'06 requirements)
- Optional for private company
- Role depends on size and nature of company (directors' meetings, registers, filing documents)
- Implied authority for administrative operations, **excluding**
  - Buying land
  - Borrowing
  - Acts usually undertaken by directors

Company records

1 Register of members

2 Register of directors and company secretary

3 Register of directors' residential addresses (protected information)

4 Register of people with significant control

5 Copies of directors' service contracts and indemnity provisions

6 Records of resolutions and minutes of members' and directors' meetings (for 10 years)

7 Directors' statement

8 Auditor's report

9 Register of charges, copies of charges

- Hard copy or electronic form
- At registered office or other place specified in regulations
- Act has rules re inspection and copies for members and others
- Contravention is offence punishable by fine

Alert! Register of debenture holders not compulsory, but if one is kept, it must comply with provisions re availability for inspection

5: Companies: the consequences of incorporation

Accounts and reports

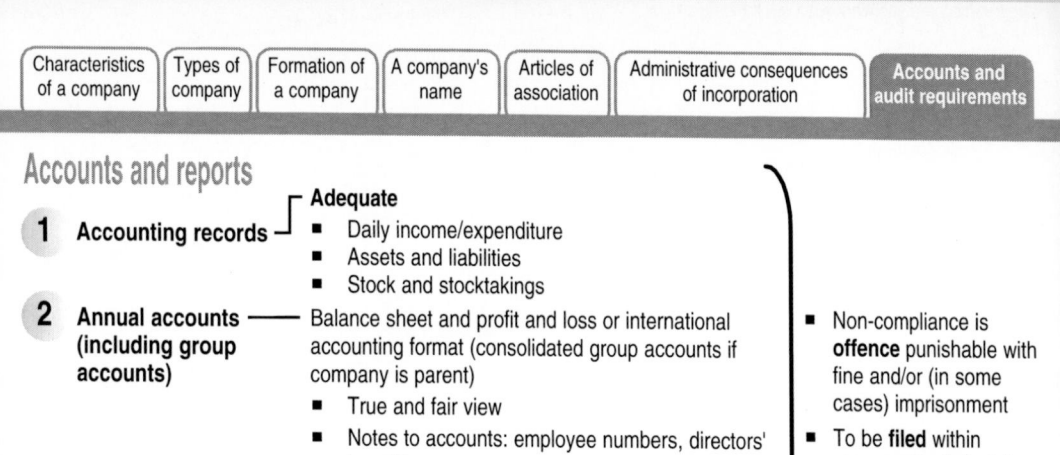

1 Accounting records — **Adequate**
- Daily income/expenditure
- Assets and liabilities
- Stock and stocktakings

2 Annual accounts (including group accounts) — Balance sheet and profit and loss or international accounting format (consolidated group accounts if company is parent)
- True and fair view
- Notes to accounts: employee numbers, directors' benefits
- Approved and signed on behalf of board

3 Directors' Report (including consolidated report) — Names
Principal activities
Auditor not unaware of relevant audit information
— Recommended dividend and business review (usually)
— Approved and signed on behalf of board

- Non-compliance is **offence** punishable with fine and/or (in some cases) imprisonment
- To be **filed** within nine months (private) six months (public) of end of relevant accounting reference period
- **Abbreviated accounts** only for small/medium companies (see below)

4 **Directors'** —— Quoted companies only
Remuneration —— Members' approval
Report

5 **Auditor's Report**
- Identify accounts and financial reporting framework
- Describe scope of audit
- Opinion that true and fair view
- State directors' report consistent with accounts

6 **Strategic Review** —— Balanced and comprehensive analysis of the development and performance of the company's business during the financial year, and the position of the company's business at the end of that year, consistent with the size and complexity of the business

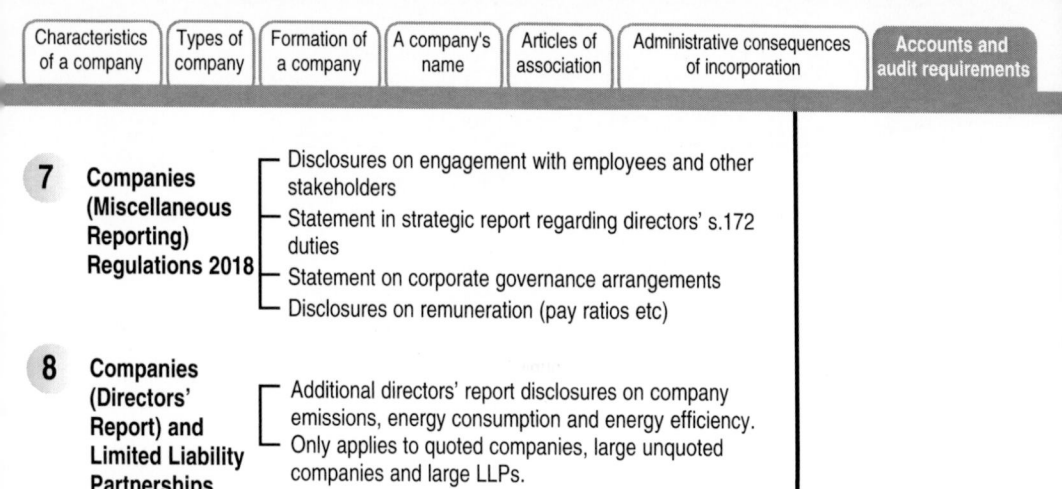

7 **Companies (Miscellaneous Reporting) Regulations 2018**
- Disclosures on engagement with employees and other stakeholders
- Statement in strategic report regarding directors' s.172 duties
- Statement on corporate governance arrangements
- Disclosures on remuneration (pay ratios etc)

8 **Companies (Directors' Report) and Limited Liability Partnerships (Energy and Carbon Report) Regulations 2018**
- Additional directors' report disclosures on company emissions, energy consumption and energy efficiency.
- Only applies to quoted companies, large unquoted companies and large LLPs.

Micro-entities and small or medium companies

	Micro	Small	Medium
Turnover	≤ £632k	≤ £10.2m	≤ £36m
Balance sheet	≤ £316k	≤ £5.1m	≤ £18m
Employees	≤ 10	≤ 50	≤ 250

1 **Abbreviated accounts** —— If satisfy two or more of the above requirements

2 **Exempt from audit**
- All micro-entities and small companies, satisfying turnover and balance sheet requirements above
- Dormant companies
- Non-profit making companies subject to public sector audit

Despite exemption, audit can be required by ≥10% members or members representing ≥10% nominal value of issued share capital

3 **Minimum accounting requirements** —— Micro-entities provide minimal information in their financial statements and do not have to follow all accounting standards

Auditors

- Appointed by directors/ordinary resolution/Secretary of State
- Those appointing should fix remuneration
- Right of access to books and accounts
- Duty to investigate
- Removal by ordinary resolution with special notice
- Offence if auditor's report misleading or false

Notes

6: Companies: ownership and management

Chapter 6 considers the balance in a company between the owners on the one hand (the members) and the managers on the other (the directors).

It explains how directors are appointed and removed and their authority to bind the company. It also describes their duties owed to the company and considers the consequences of any breach or fraudulent or wrongful trading, including disqualification. In considering the members of a company, the chapter describes those actions by directors that require the approval of the members in general meeting and then goes on to consider how minority shareholders can take action in certain circumstances, notwithstanding the general principle of company law that the will of the majority prevails.

The last section deals with the various statutory rules regulating meetings and resolutions within the framework of registered companies.

Director

Any person who occupies the position or fulfils the role of director, whatever they are called

- At least one (private) two (public)
- Age $\geq$ 16 years old
- No upper age limit

1 **Appointed director**
- By ordinary resolution
- By existing directors

2 **De facto director** — Anyone who acts as director
  - Same powers and liabilities

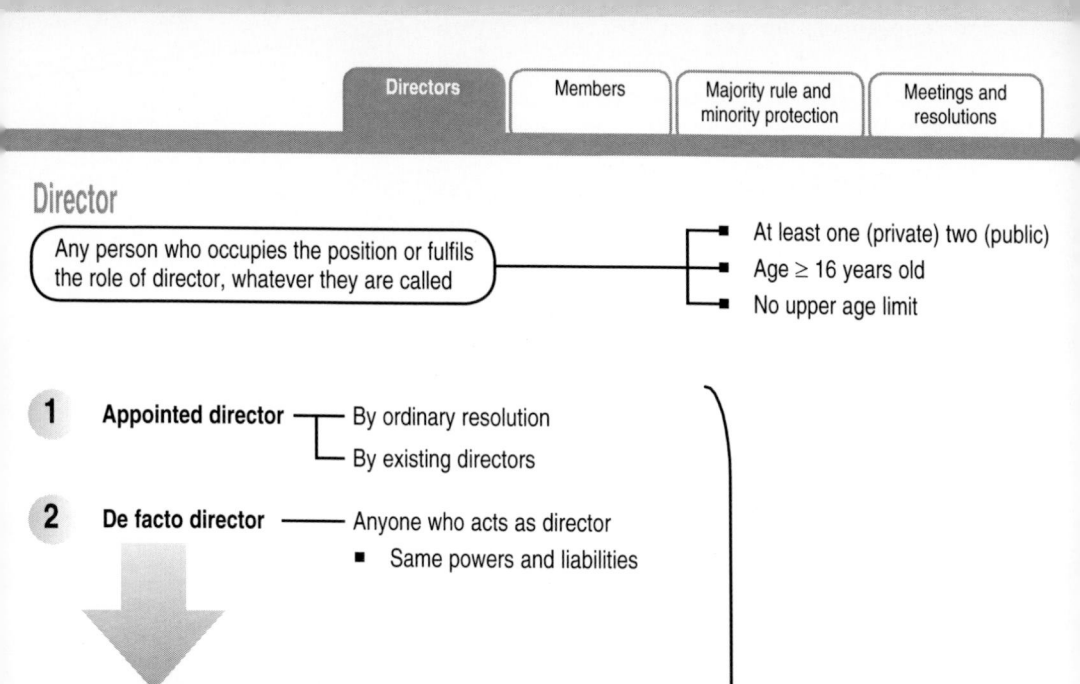

3 **Shadow director** ——— Someone in accordance with whose directions or instructions the directors are accustomed to act
- Question of fact

4 **Alternate director** ——— Appointed by director as 'stand-in'
- Director/outsider

5 **Executive** ——— Specific role

6 **Non-executive** ——— No specific role

7 **MD** ——— Executive
- Day-to-day management

- Actions valid notwithstanding defective appointment
- Notify any change within 14 days
- All owe directors' duties
- Companies Act 2006 does not distinguish between types of director – either a person is a director or is not

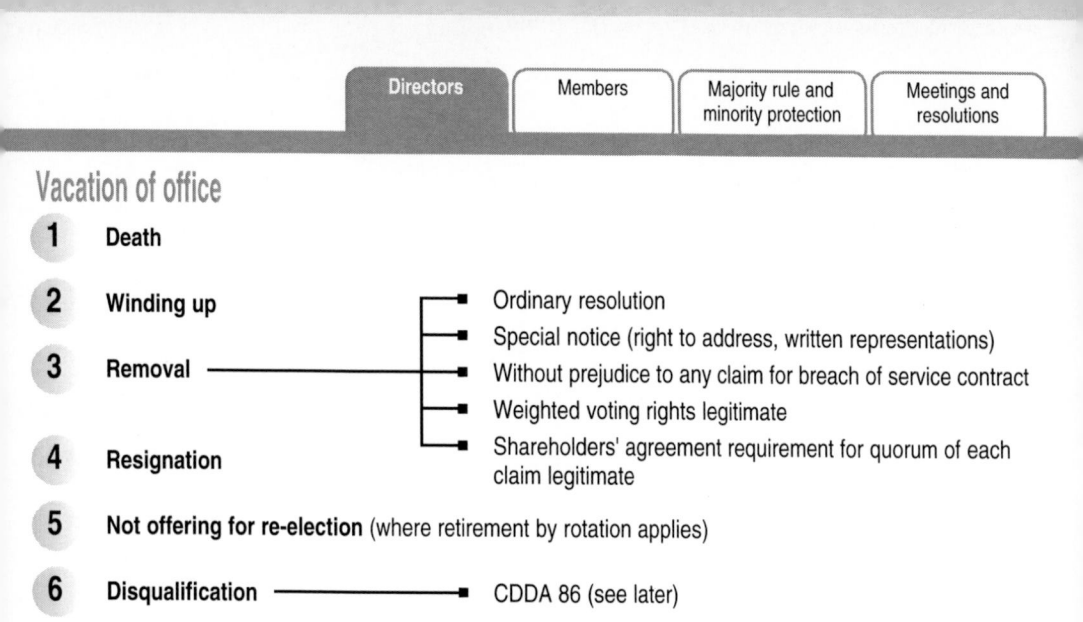

Vacation of office

1 **Death**

2 **Winding up**

3 **Removal**
- Ordinary resolution
- Special notice (right to address, written representations)
- Without prejudice to any claim for breach of service contract
- Weighted voting rights legitimate
- Shareholders' agreement requirement for quorum of each claim legitimate

4 **Resignation**

5 **Not offering for re-election** (where retirement by rotation applies)

6 **Disqualification** — CDDA 86 (see later)

7 **Articles, eg**
- Unsound mind
- Bankruptcy

Directors' powers

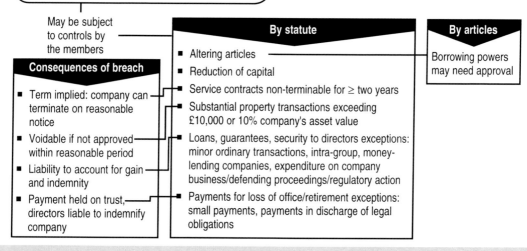

Vested in directors as collective body to exercise in board meetings – to manage the business of the company and to exercise all the powers of the company

Duty to exercise powers for purpose conferred

May be subject to controls by the members

By statute

- Altering articles
- Reduction of capital
- Service contracts non-terminable for ≥ two years
- Substantial property transactions exceeding £10,000 or 10% company's asset value
- Loans, guarantees, security to directors exceptions: minor ordinary transactions, intra-group, money-lending companies, expenditure on company business/defending proceedings/regulatory action
- Payments for loss of office/retirement exceptions: small payments, payments in discharge of legal obligations

By articles

Borrowing powers may need approval

Consequences of breach

- Term implied: company can terminate on reasonable notice
- Voidable if not approved within reasonable period
- Liability to account for gain and indemnity
- Payment held on trust, directors liable to indemnify company

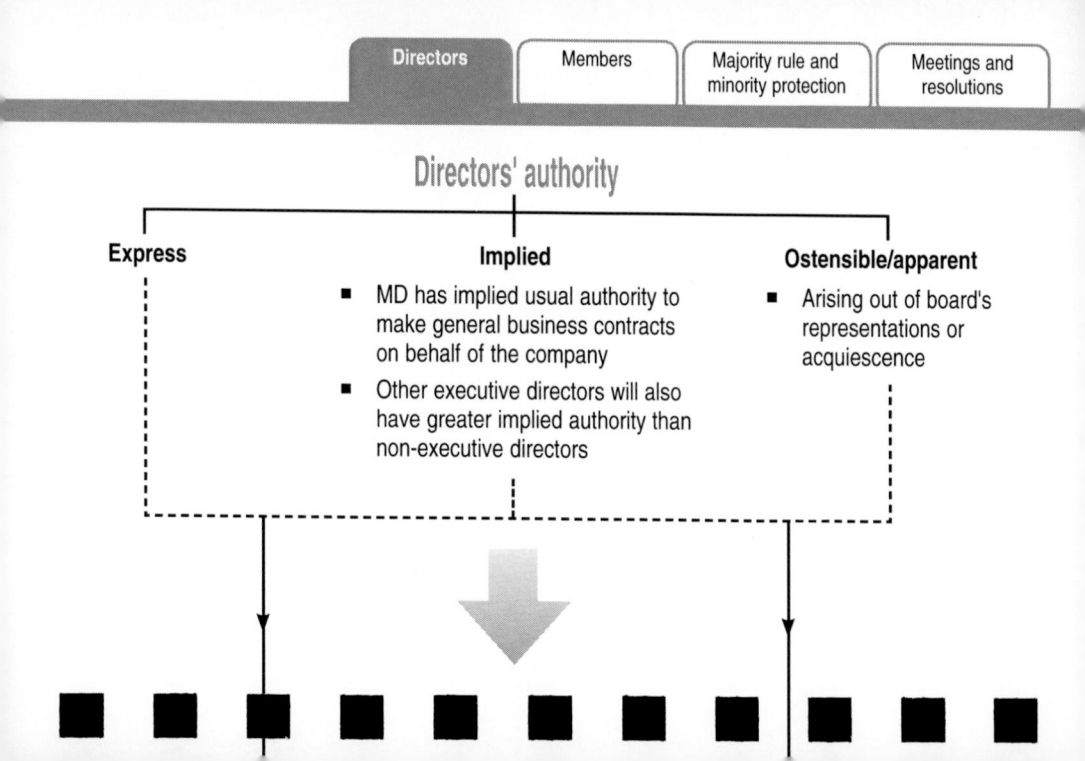

Directors' authority

Express

Implied

- MD has implied usual authority to make general business contracts on behalf of the company
- Other executive directors will also have greater implied authority than non-executive directors

Ostensible/apparent

- Arising out of board's representations or acquiescence

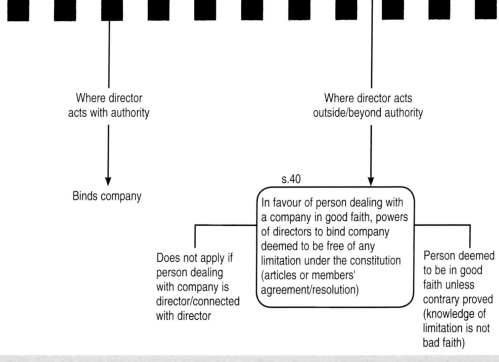

Where director
acts with authority

Where director acts
outside/beyond authority

Binds company

s.40

In favour of person dealing with
a company in good faith, powers
of directors to bind company
deemed to be free of any
limitation under the constitution
(articles or members'
agreement/resolution)

Does not apply if
person dealing
with company is
director/connected
with director

Person deemed
to be in good
faith unless
contrary proved
(knowledge of
limitation is not
bad faith)

Directors' duties

1 Act within powers
- Within constitution
- For purpose conferred

■ If act for collateral purpose, then action invalid **unless**
- Approved
- Ratified

By the company in general meeting

Approval/ratification

On 'irregular' allotment of shares: votes on new shares cannot count

2 Act in good faith, to promote success of company for benefit of members as a whole

Having regard to
- Long term consequences
- Employees' interests
- Fostering business relationships
- Community and environment
- Reputation for business conduct
- Fairness between members

Note

Also subject to any requirement to consider interests of creditors

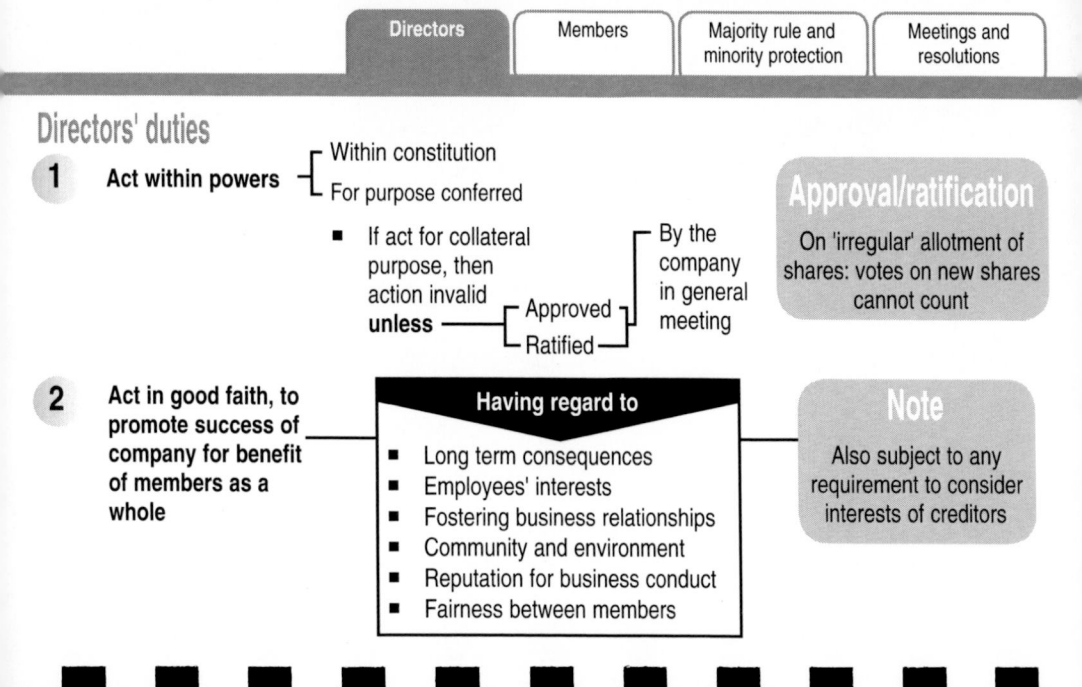

3 **Exercise independent judgment**

No breach if acts in accordance with
— Constitution
— Lawful agreement

4 **Exercise reasonable care, skill and diligence**

By reasonably diligent person with
— General knowledge, skill and experience of person performing their functions as director,
and
— Specific knowledge, skill and experience of director concerned

Remember!

A director who signs insurance proposal without reading it likely to be in breach

Remember!

Attending board meetings and nothing more, likely to be in breach, especially if executive or non-executive with some business experience

5 **Avoid conflict of interest**
- Re exploitation of property, information or opportunity

— No breach if authorised by **directors**
- Private: unless constitution prohibits
- Public: constitution must allow
- Director not included in quorum
- Directors' votes not count

— If members' approval needed under other provision, directors' authorisation **not** also needed

6 **Declare interest in transaction/ arrangement** to directors (unless no conflict)

— Disclosure notice
- Board meeting or
- In writing or
- General notice

Alert! No approval needed, disclosure sufficient

— **Unless** other provision requires members' approval (constitution/ substantial non-cash asset)

7 **Not to accept benefits from third parties** (unless no conflict)

— By reason of being/acting as director

Consequences of breach

- Joint and several liability
- Injunction if before breach
- Make good losses
- Account for secret profits
- Contracts voidable
- Property recoverable from director (and third party unless acquired for value in good faith)

Articles

Cannot dilute statutory duties but can impose more onerous duties

Ratification

Of breach is possible by ordinary resolution, disregarding votes of director(s) in breach

Exclusion of liability for breach

Void, except company can provide insurance or qualifying indemnity re third parties

Most likely court action for breach = derivative action (s.260)
(see later)

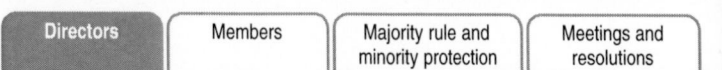

Wrongful trading

> Director(s) knew or should have known no reasonable prospect of company avoiding insolvent liquidation and did not take sufficient steps to minimise potential loss to creditors

- Civil offence
- Arises in liquidation only
- Reasonably diligent person with general knowledge, skill and experience reasonably expected of person carrying out their director-duties **and** their own specific knowledge, skill and experience
- Liability to contribute to company's assets as court sees fit
- Directors only

Fraudulent trading

> Where company's business is carried on with intent to defraud creditors (of company or another) or for any fraudulent purpose

- Anyone 'knowingly a party', actively involved
- Single transactions included

Civil

- In liquidation only
- To contribute to company's assets as court sees fit

Criminal

- Liquidation **or** while going concern
- Fine and/or up to 10 years

- Can also be committed by non-corporate trader

Breach of disqualification order

Can result in fine and/or imprisonment

From being a director, liquidator, administrator, receiver or manager and from being concerned in the promotion or management of any company

Discretionary up to **15 years**

- Conviction for serious offence
- Fraudulent trading (conviction not necessary)
- Public interest
- Certain breaches of competition law
- Wrongful trading

Note:

- Ordinary commercial misjudgment – **insufficient**
- Lack of commercial probity, gross negligence or total incompetence – **sufficient**

Discretionary up to **5 years**

- Persistent default of company legislation (3 convictions in 5 years conclusive)

Mitigating circumstances

- Lack of dishonesty
- Loss of director's own money
- Absence of personal gain
- Efforts to mitigate
- Reoffending unlikely

Mandatory **2–15 years**

- Also director of a company that has become insolvent at any time
  and
- Conduct as director of that company makes them unfit to be concerned in management of a company

Note:

Bankruptcy order = Automatic disqualification

6: Companies: ownership and management

Member

Subscribers and any person entered on the company's register of members (also a 'shareholder' if owns shares in the company)

Shareholder's agreement

- May offer more protection to members
- Not require registration, therefore privacy (eg, banking details, confidentiality, undertakings, etc)
- Enforceable contract
- Common to quasi-partnerships

Members' rights

- To be sent copy accounts/reports
- To require directors to call general meeting
- To appoint a proxy
- To vote

Member may enforce personal rights in a **personal action**

Company may send communications in **electronic** form subject to

- Constitution
- Member's agreement (general or specific)

Member of **listed company** holding shares for another may nominate that person to enjoy information rights

- Electronic form acceptable unless hard copies requested

Remember!

Members' approval required of certain actions:

- Service contracts fixed $\geq$ two years
- Substantial property transactions
- Loans etc, to directors
- Payments for loss of office

Majority rule *(Foss v Harbottle)*

Will of majority prevails. Usually minority has no recourse because company (acting in general meeting) is proper claimant

Minority action

| Statutory rights | Derivative action (s.260) | Petition for unfairly prejudicial conduct | Just and equitable winding up |

Statutory rights

1 Variation of class rights cancellation (15%)

2 Requisition general meeting (10%)

3 Notice of members' resolution (5%)

4 Court application to prohibit payment out of capital (any member)

5 Re-registration as unlimited company (any member)

Derivative action (s.260)

- Negligence or breach of duty
- Wrongdoing directors not necessarily majority
- Member must make prima facie case
  - Case refusal if ┬ Authorisation
    ├ Ratification
    └ Person promoting success would not agree

Factors

- Good faith?
- Importance? in eyes of promoter of success
- Authorisation/ratification likely?
- Any company decision?
- Could member have personal claim?
- Views of objective members

Defence

Court may excuse director acting honestly and reasonably and who, having regard to all circumstances, ought fairly to be excused

Petition for unfairly prejudicial conduct

- Any member/Sec. State
- U.P. to members generally or some part, **as member(s)**
- Past/present/future conduct
- Concerns **effect** of conduct, not motive etc

- Petitioner's conduct relevant
- Breach of company law not essential but makes successful claim more likely

Examples

- ☑ Exclusion in quasi-partnership
- ☑ Improper allotment
- ☑ Misleading shareholders
- ☑ Diverting business to director business
- ☒ Parent not paying subsidiary's debts
- ☒ Non-compliance with Stock Exchange Rules

Orders

- Regulation of company affairs
- Authorisation of legal proceedings
- Requiring company to do/not do something
- Purchase of minority shares
- Alter/not alter articles

Most common relief

Fair value
- Disregard that minority holding
- Worth before unfair conduct

Just and equitable winding up

- Show no other remedy available
  (remedy of last resort)

Examples

- Illegal/fraudulent purpose

- Deadlock

- Directors withholding information,
  leading to loss of confidence in
  management

6: Companies: ownership and management

Meetings

General
- Called by — Directors
  — Members
  — Court
  — Auditor

- **Must** be called when net assets fall ≤ 50% called up capital (public only)

Requisition

5% paid up capital with voting rights, or
5% of voting rights

- Directors 21 days to call meeting
- 28 days notice
- If fail, requisitioning members (or 50% voting rights) may call, within three months of initial request

AGM
- Only public company required to have AGM
- Within six months of accounting reference date
- Failure punishable by fine
- Accounts and reports to be laid before AGM (also dividends, appointment of directors/auditors)

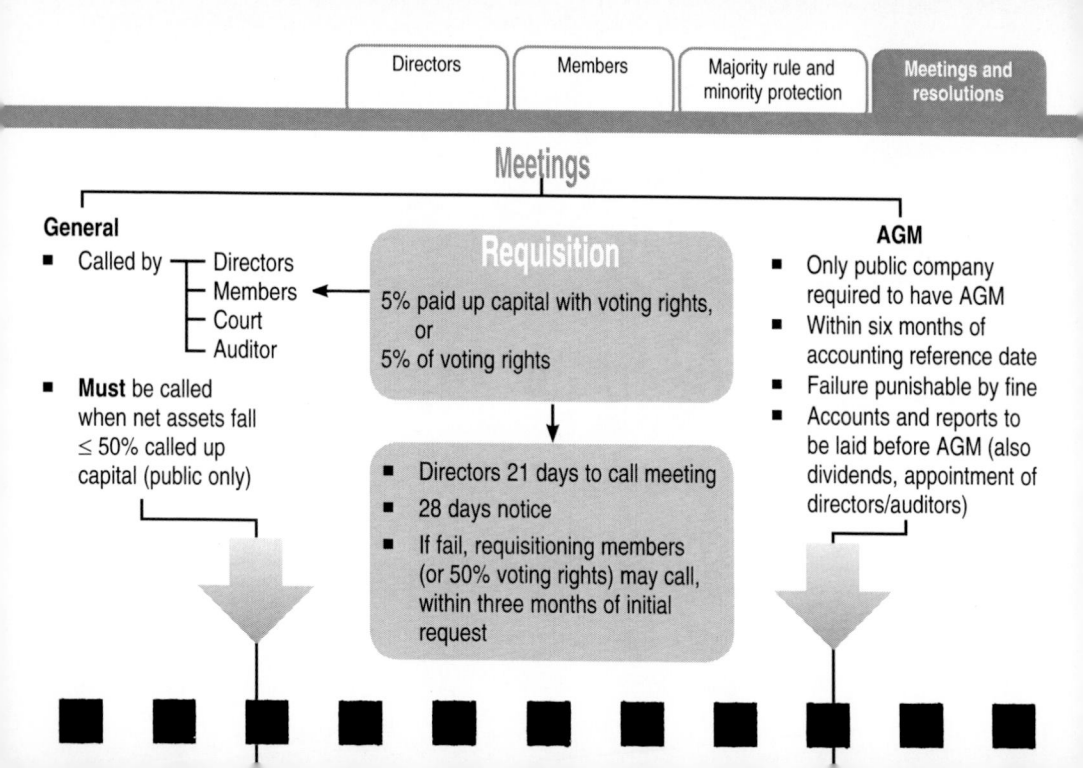

Notice (general)

- 14 **clear** days' notice (shorter if 90%)
- To every member and director giving time, date, place and general nature of business

Notice (AGM)

- 21 **clear** days' notice (shorter if 100%)
- Must state AGM
- Resolution may be demanded by 5% or 100 shareholders with average ≥ £100

Special notice

28 days; required for resolution to remove auditor or director, who may require to be heard and have written representations circulated

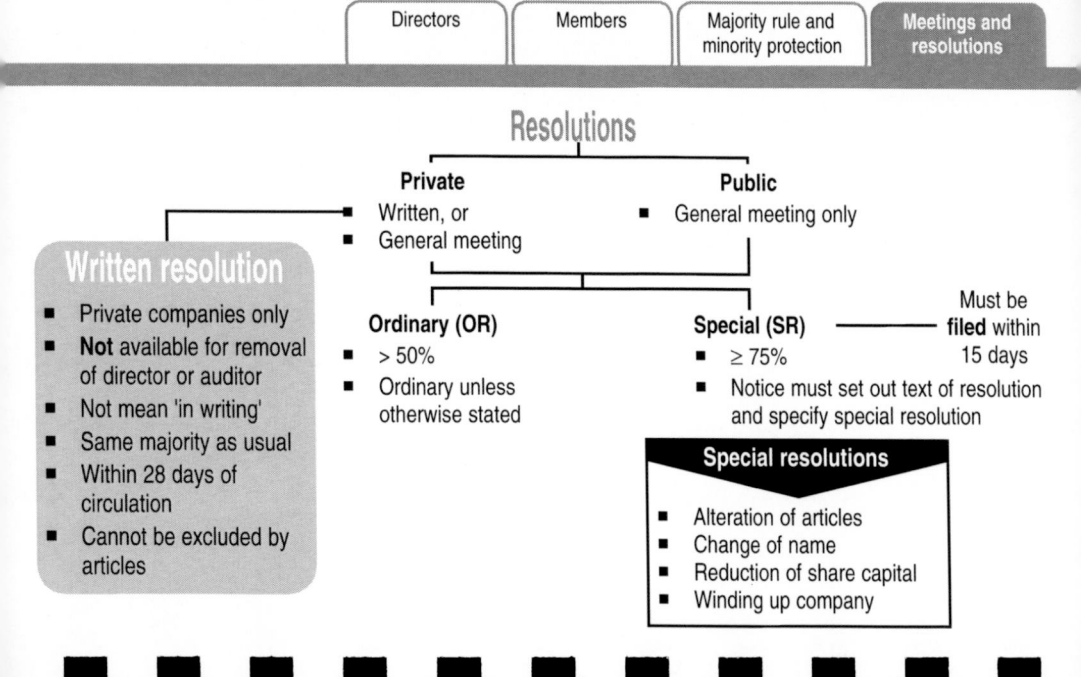

Resolutions

Private
- Written, or
- General meeting

Public
- General meeting only

Written resolution
- Private companies only
- **Not** available for removal of director or auditor
- Not mean 'in writing'
- Same majority as usual
- Within 28 days of circulation
- Cannot be excluded by articles

Ordinary (OR)
- > 50%
- Ordinary unless otherwise stated

Special (SR)
- ≥ 75%
- Notice must set out text of resolution and specify special resolution

Must be **filed** within 15 days

Special resolutions
- Alteration of articles
- Change of name
- Reduction of share capital
- Winding up company

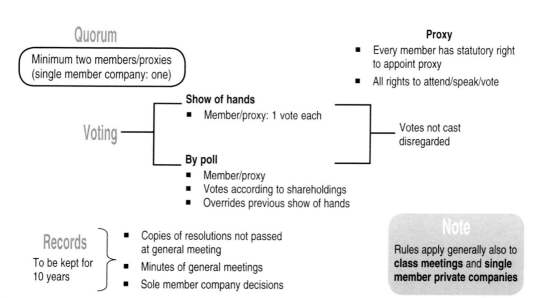

Quorum

Minimum two members/proxies
(single member company: one)

Proxy
- Every member has statutory right to appoint proxy
- All rights to attend/speak/vote

Voting

Show of hands
- Member/proxy: 1 vote each

By poll
- Member/proxy
- Votes according to shareholdings
- Overrides previous show of hands

Votes not cast
disregarded

Records

To be kept for 10 years

- Copies of resolutions not passed at general meeting
- Minutes of general meetings
- Sole member company decisions

Note

Rules apply generally also to **class meetings** and **single member private companies**

Notes

7: Companies: finance

This chapter explores the financing of companies limited by shares. It describes the principal types of share and how they are allotted and transferred. The rules on payment for shares, rights of pre-emption and dividends are included. The principle of maintenance of capital is explained and the rules on redemption and purchase of shares and financial assistance are described.

It also considers the raising of capital by loan agreements and examines fixed and floating charges offered as security for a company's borrowing.

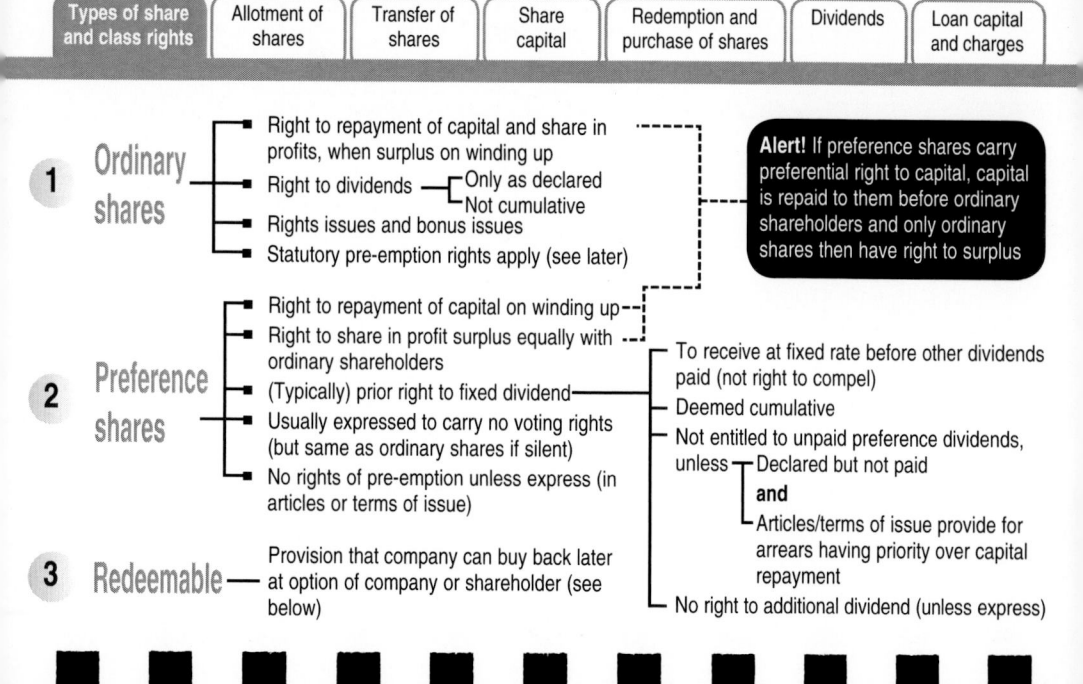

1 Ordinary shares

- Right to repayment of capital and share in profits, when surplus on winding up
- Right to dividends — Only as declared / Not cumulative
- Rights issues and bonus issues
- Statutory pre-emption rights apply (see later)

Alert! If preference shares carry preferential right to capital, capital is repaid to them before ordinary shareholders and only ordinary shares then have right to surplus

2 Preference shares

- Right to repayment of capital on winding up
- Right to share in profit surplus equally with ordinary shareholders
- (Typically) prior right to fixed dividend
- Usually expressed to carry no voting rights (but same as ordinary shares if silent)
- No rights of pre-emption unless express (in articles or terms of issue)

- To receive at fixed rate before other dividends paid (not right to compel)
- Deemed cumulative
- Not entitled to unpaid preference dividends, unless — Declared but not paid **and** Articles/terms of issue provide for arrears having priority over capital repayment
- No right to additional dividend (unless express)

3 Redeemable — Provision that company can buy back later at option of company or shareholder (see below)

Class rights

Identical rights attached to shares in one class that are different from rights enjoyed by other shareholders

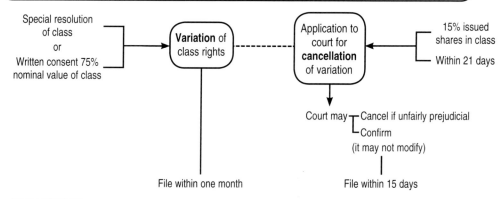

Special resolution
of class
or
Written consent 75%
nominal value of class

→ **Variation** of class rights

Application to court for **cancellation** of variation

15% issued shares in class

Within 21 days

File within one month

Court may ┌ Cancel if unfairly prejudicial
          └ Confirm
          (it may not modify)

File within 15 days

Alert!
The rights themselves must be altered – there is no variation just because existing rights are affected. *(Greenhalgh)*

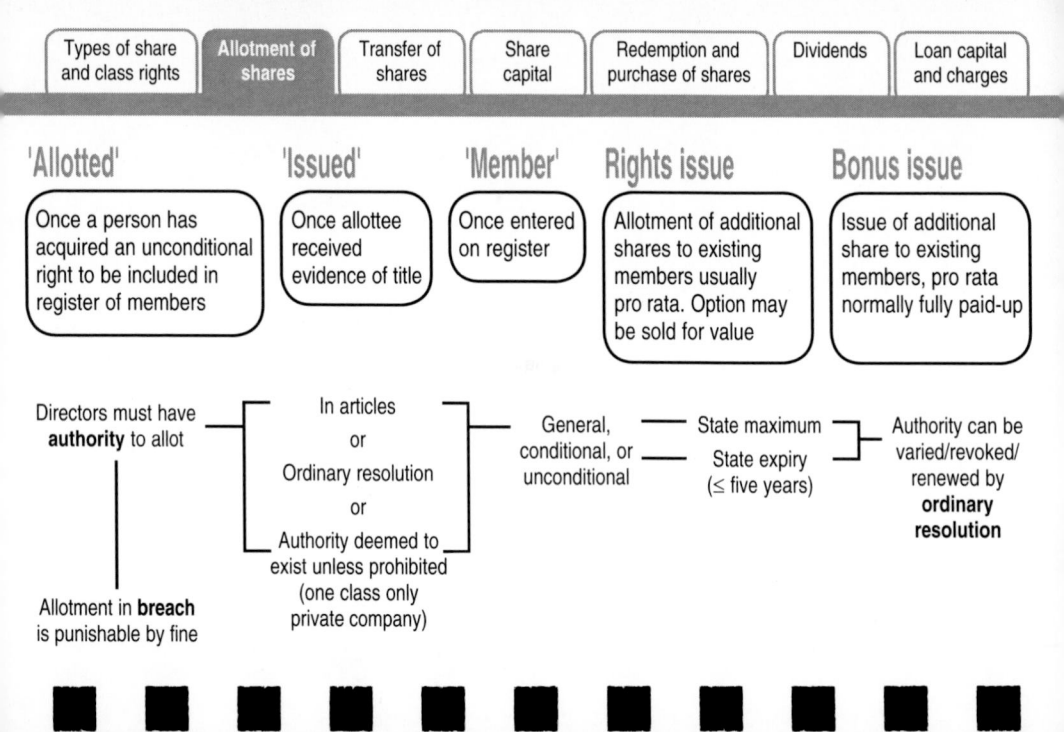

'Allotted'

Once a person has acquired an unconditional right to be included in register of members

'Issued'

Once allottee received evidence of title

'Member'

Once entered on register

Rights issue

Allotment of additional shares to existing members usually pro rata. Option may be sold for value

Bonus issue

Issue of additional share to existing members, pro rata normally fully paid-up

Directors must have **authority** to allot

Allotment in **breach** is punishable by fine

In articles

or

Ordinary resolution

or

Authority deemed to exist unless prohibited (one class only private company)

General, conditional, or unconditional

State maximum

State expiry (≤ five years)

Authority can be varied/revoked/renewed by **ordinary resolution**

Allotment may need to be made in accordance with **statutory rights of pre-emption**

> Equity securities (usually ordinary shares for cash) to be offered to existing shareholders in proportion to existing shareholdings on same/more favourable terms

Allotment in breach
- Still valid, but
- Compensation available for two years

Written/electronic offer, give 21 days for acceptance —— If not accepted, may be allotted to non-members

Statutory rights do NOT apply

1 Bonus shares

2 Non-cash consideration

3 Employees' share scheme

4 Authority may be given to allot without applying rights by
- Articles
- or
- Special resolution

5 If excluded by articles (private only)

6 Private one class only: if disapplied by
- Articles
- or
- Special resolution

7: Companies: finance

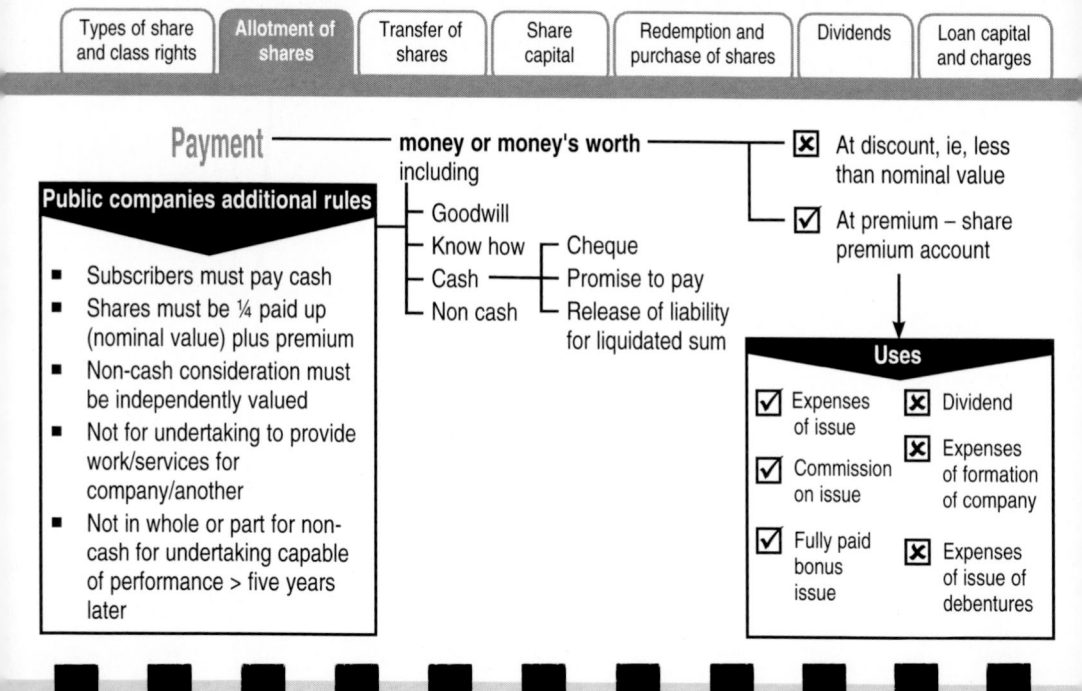

Payment — **money or money's worth** including

- Goodwill
- Know how
- Cash —— Cheque / Promise to pay / Release of liability for liquidated sum
- Non cash

Public companies additional rules

- Subscribers must pay cash
- Shares must be ¼ paid up (nominal value) plus premium
- Non-cash consideration must be independently valued
- Not for undertaking to provide work/services for company/another
- Not in whole or part for non-cash for undertaking capable of performance > five years later

- ☒ At discount, ie, less than nominal value
- ☑ At premium – share premium account

Uses

- ☑ Expenses of issue
- ☑ Commission on issue
- ☑ Fully paid bonus issue
- ☒ Dividend
- ☒ Expenses of formation of company
- ☒ Expenses of issue of debentures

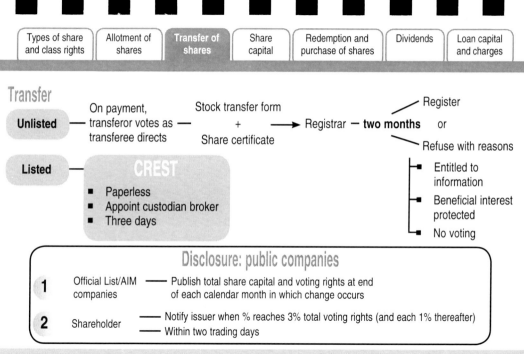

Transfer

Unlisted — On payment, transferor votes as transferee directs

Stock transfer form + Share certificate → Registrar — **two months** — Register or Refuse with reasons

- Entitled to information
- Beneficial interest protected
- No voting

Listed —

CREST

- Paperless
- Appoint custodian broker
- Three days

Disclosure: public companies

1 Official List/AIM companies — Publish total share capital and voting rights at end of each calendar month in which change occurs

2 Shareholder — Notify issuer when % reaches 3% total voting rights (and each 1% thereafter)
— Within two trading days

Company having share capital

Company with power to issue shares

Public company: authorised minimum requirement £50,000

Issued/allotted share capital

Includes shares taken by subscribers

Equity share capital

Issued share capital **excluding** any part (re dividend or capital) with right to participate beyond specified amount in a distribution

Called-up share capital

Amount of calls made on shares
+
Shares paid up without being called
+
Share capital to be paid at specified later date

Alteration of share capital

- [x] Generally, cannot reduce capital (see below)
- [x] Increase – allot more shares
- [x] Subdivide (OR)
- [x] Consolidate (OR)
- [x] Redenomination (reduction subject to 10% limit and SR)

Maintenance of capital: General rule that share capital should not be reduced/returned

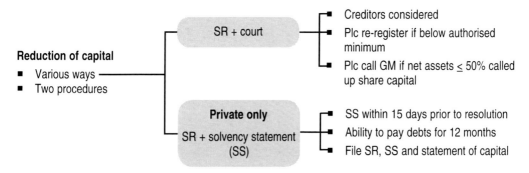

Reduction of capital
- Various ways
- Two procedures

SR + court
- Creditors considered
- Plc re-register if below authorised minimum
- Plc call GM if net assets ≤ 50% called up share capital

Private only
SR + solvency statement (SS)
- SS within 15 days prior to resolution
- Ability to pay debts for 12 months
- File SR, SS and statement of capital

REDEMPTION

- Must be non-redeemable shares in issue
- Shares must be fully paid
- Payment on redemption
- Redeemed shares treated as cancelled

Authority
- Plc: articles must give
- Private: articles may exclude/restrict

Note: **Or** may give authority despite change to articles

Funds
- Distributable profits (diminution in issued share capital goes to capital redemption reserve)
- Proceeds of fresh issue
- **Private only** capital
  - SR
  - Directors' statement
  - Auditor's report
  - Publicity

Payment
- 5–7 weeks after resolution

Notice
- Notice of redemption and statement of capital to be filed within one month

PURCHASE OF OWN SHARES

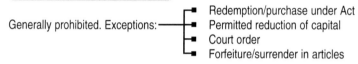

Generally prohibited. Exceptions:
- Redemption/purchase under Act
- Permitted reduction of capital
- Court order
- Forfeiture/surrender in articles

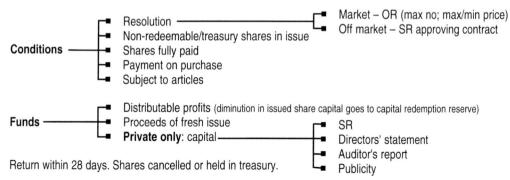

Conditions
- Resolution
  - Market – OR (max no; max/min price)
  - Off market – SR approving contract
- Non-redeemable/treasury shares in issue
- Shares fully paid
- Payment on purchase
- Subject to articles

Funds
- Distributable profits (diminution in issued share capital goes to capital redemption reserve)
- Proceeds of fresh issue
- **Private only**: capital
  - SR
  - Directors' statement
  - Auditor's report
  - Publicity

Return within 28 days. Shares cancelled or held in treasury.

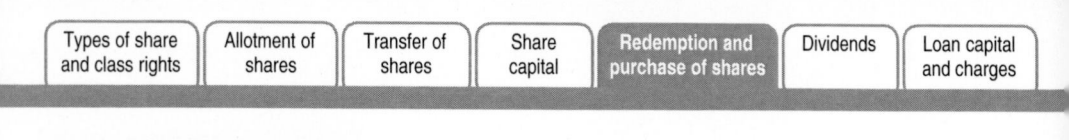

FINANCIAL ASSISTANCE (FA)

Public company: FA in company or holding company must be in good faith in company's interests and ⎯⎯⎯

- Either principal purpose is other than acquisition

  or

- FA only an incidental part of other purpose

Permitted FA: ⎯⎯⎯
- Lending = ordinary business
- Employees' share scheme
- Loans to employees for fully paid shares

Private ☑
Public ☑ Provided ⎯⎯
- Net assets Not reduced

  or

- FA given from distributable profits

Breach of FA rules ⎯⎯⎯
- Criminal offence (fine and/or imprisonment)
- Civil consequences (directors' liability and validity of contracts)

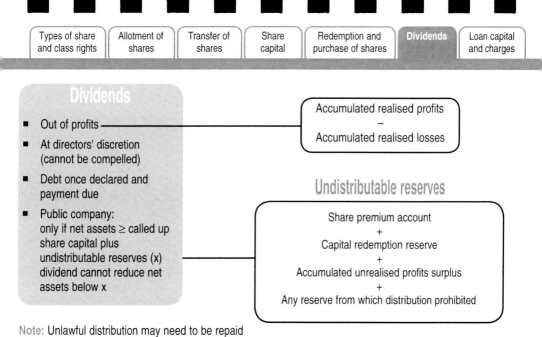

Dividends

- Out of profits ——————————————

  Accumulated realised profits
  −
  Accumulated realised losses

- At directors' discretion (cannot be compelled)

- Debt once declared and payment due

Undistributable reserves

- Public company:
  only if net assets ≥ called up share capital plus undistributable reserves (x) dividend cannot reduce net assets below x

  Share premium account
  +
  Capital redemption reserve
  +
  Accumulated unrealised profits surplus
  +
  Any reserve from which distribution prohibited

Note: Unlawful distribution may need to be repaid

Debenture

A written acknowledgement of a debt by a company, whether or not secured by a **charge**

Floating charge

Charge on a class of assets, present and/or future, ordinarily changing from time to time and with which company can continue to deal until charge enforced

Debentureholder	Shareholder
Creditor	Member
☒ No voting rights	☑ Voting rights
☑ Discounts possible	☒ No discount
Right to interest when due	Right to return only when dividend declared
☑ Redemption permitted	☒ Redemption restricted
Paid before shareholders on liquidation	Paid after debentureholders

Crystallisation	Floating charge	Fixed charge
■ Liquidation	Attaches on crystallisation	Attaches on creation
■ Cessation of business	Company **can** deal without consent	Company **cannot** deal without consent
■ Chargee's intervention		
■ Specified event, eg, breach	Avoidable as preference: 12 months	Avoidable as preference: 6 months

Fixed or floating

Label not conclusive

Test = can company deal without consent? If so, floating

Reservation of title clause

> Whereby creditor sells and delivers goods to the company, on condition that they retain legal ownership until the debt is paid

Negative pledge clause

> Prohibition, contained in a floating charge, against the company creating subsequent fixed charge with priority

Priority

1st	2nd	(3rd)	Priority (provided registered)
Fixed	Fixed		First fixed
Fixed	Floating		Fixed
Floating	Fixed		Fixed
Floating with negative pledge clause	Fixed		Floating
Floating	Fixed	Floating charge crystallises	Fixed

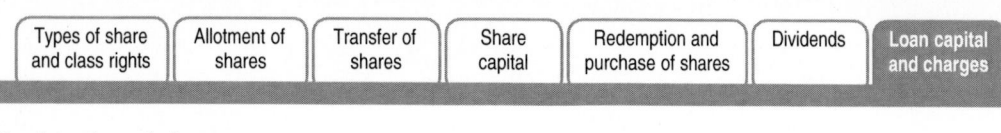

Registration of charges

1 Company must keep copies of charge

2 Company's register of charges, showing
- Name of chargee
- Amount of charge
- Property charged

At registered office or another place Notified to Registrar

3 File within **21 days** → Registrar issues certificate of registration (conclusive evidence of compliance)

→ Breach punishable by fine and renders charge **void** against liquidator/administrator/company

8: Insolvency law: corporate and personal

Topic List

Administration

Receivership

Liquidation

Individual voluntary arrangements

Bankruptcy

Chapter 8 begins by examining three principal procedures relevant to a company in financial difficulty, in particular administration (aimed at rescuing the company as a going concern) and liquidation (the process for winding up a company's business). It then goes on to describe how an individual may be declared bankrupt and how individual voluntary arrangements may provide an appropriate alternative to bankruptcy.

Purpose of administration (in order)

1 To rescue company as a going concern

2 To achieve a better result for creditors as a whole, than would be likely with a winding-up

3 To realise the company's assets to make a distribution to one or more preferential or secured creditors, provided administrator does not 'unnecessarily harm' the interests of the creditors as a whole

Qualifying floating charge holder ('QFCH')

Floating charge holder with a floating charge that, on its own or together with other fixed or floating charges, amounts to a charge over the whole or substantially the whole of the company's assets and that contains power to appoint an administrator

Administrator's statement

Statement that   (a) purpose of administration is likely to be achieved; and
                      (b) they consent to their appointment

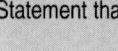

Appointment of an administrator

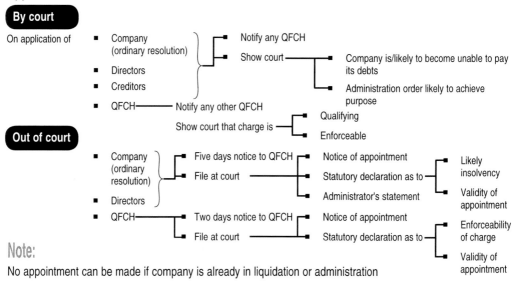

By court

On application of

- Company (ordinary resolution) —— Notify any QFCH
- Directors
- Creditors
- QFCH —— Notify any other QFCH

Show court —— Company is/likely to become unable to pay its debts

Administration order likely to achieve purpose

Show court that charge is —— Qualifying

Enforceable

Out of court

- Company (ordinary resolution)
- Directors

Five days notice to QFCH —— Notice of appointment

File at court —— Statutory declaration as to —— Likely insolvency

Validity of appointment

Administrator's statement

- QFCH —— Two days notice to QFCH —— Notice of appointment

File at court —— Statutory declaration as to —— Enforceability of charge

Validity of appointment

Note:

No appointment can be made if company is already in liquidation or administration

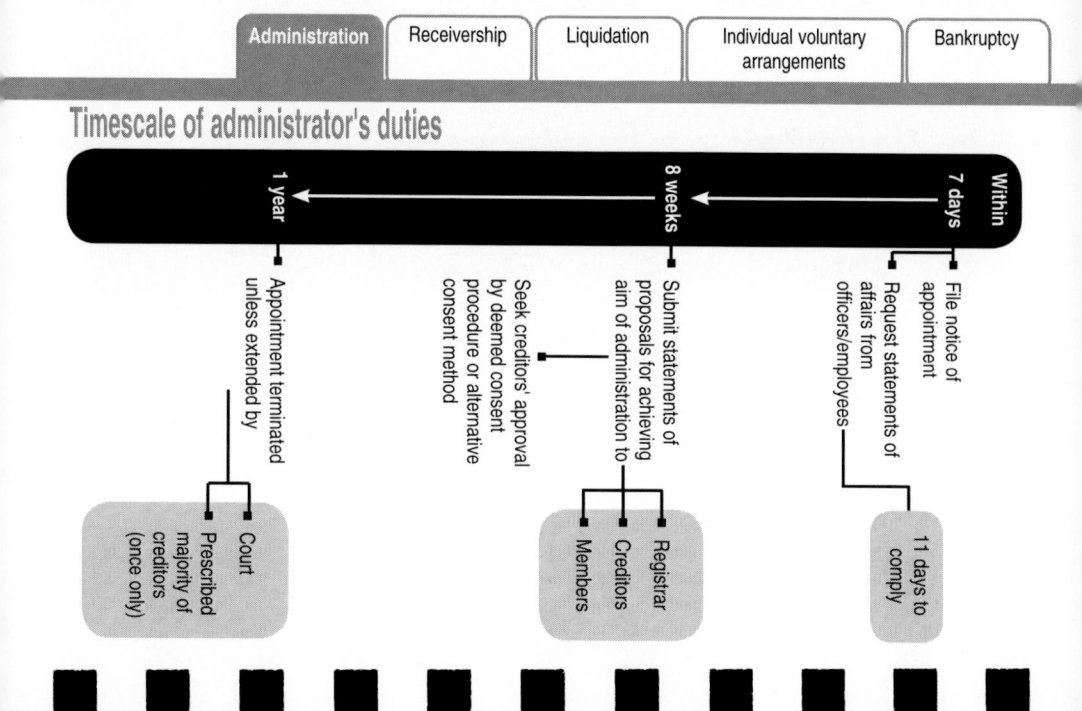

Administration | Receivership | Liquidation | Individual voluntary arrangements | Bankruptcy

Timescale of administrator's duties

Within 7 days

File notice of appointment

Request statements of affairs from officers/employees

11 days to comply

8 weeks

Submit statements of proposals for achieving aim of administration to

Registrar
Creditors
Members

Seek creditors' approval by deemed consent procedure or alternative consent method

1 year

Appointment terminated unless extended by

Court
Prescribed majority of creditors (once only)

Powers of an administrator

- Remove and appoint directors
- Dismiss employees
- Call meeting of members/creditors (if requested)
- Avoid transactions (see later)
- Apply to court for directions
- Make payments to secured/preferential creditors
- Make payments to unsecured creditors if they consider it will help to achieve purpose or with consent of court
- Present or defend petition for winding up and generally to do anything necessarily expedient for the management of the affairs, business and property of the company

Any member or creditor may apply to the court if they believe that the administrator has acted or will act in a way that has harmed or will harm their interest.

Consequences of administration

1. **Moratorium**

2. **The administrator may sell** ──
   - Property subject to a floating charge ── Using the proceeds for the business ── Without the chargee's consent
   - Assets on HP ──
   - Assets subject to a fixed charge ── Provided uses the proceeds to pay off owner or chargee ── With the court's consent

3. **Directors' powers are suspended but they remain in office unless removed**

4. **Transactions at an undervalue and preferences may be avoided** (see later)

Moratorium

- No resolution/court order to wind up company
- No enforcement of security or retention clause
- No recovery of property on HP or leasing arrangement
- No legal proceedings

Except with the consent of the administrator or court

Receivership

Secured creditor with fixed charge (usually) appoints **receiver** in the event of company's default

Receiver realises charged assets and applies proceeds to pay off secured creditor

Note

Appointment of receiver normally causes crystallisation of any floating charge

Administrative receiver

A **receiver** who also acts as manager, usually appointed by a floating chargeholder

Duties of receiver

- To act in good faith
- To act with reasonable care and diligence

Powers (in addition to those contained in charge)

- To borrow
- To take legal proceedings
- To appoint professional advisers
- To pay off creditors with preferential rights

Note

Enterprise Act 2002 generally prohibits the appointment of administrative receivers

| Administration | Receivership | **Liquidation** | Individual voluntary arrangements | Bankruptcy |

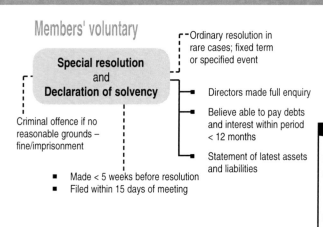

Members' voluntary

Special resolution and **Declaration of solvency**

┌ Ordinary resolution in rare cases; fixed term or specified event

- Directors made full enquiry
- Believe able to pay debts and interest within period < 12 months
- Statement of latest assets and liabilities

Criminal offence if no reasonable grounds – fine/imprisonment

- Made < 5 weeks before resolution
- Filed within 15 days of meeting

Creditors' voluntary

Special resolution (and no declaration of solvency)

↓

Procedure

- Directors nominate liquidator
- Creditors approve nomination by deemed consent procedure or alternative consent method
- Creditors must be sent statement of affairs within 7 days of the resolution to liquidate
- Creditor approval must be obtained within 14 days of the resolution to liquidate

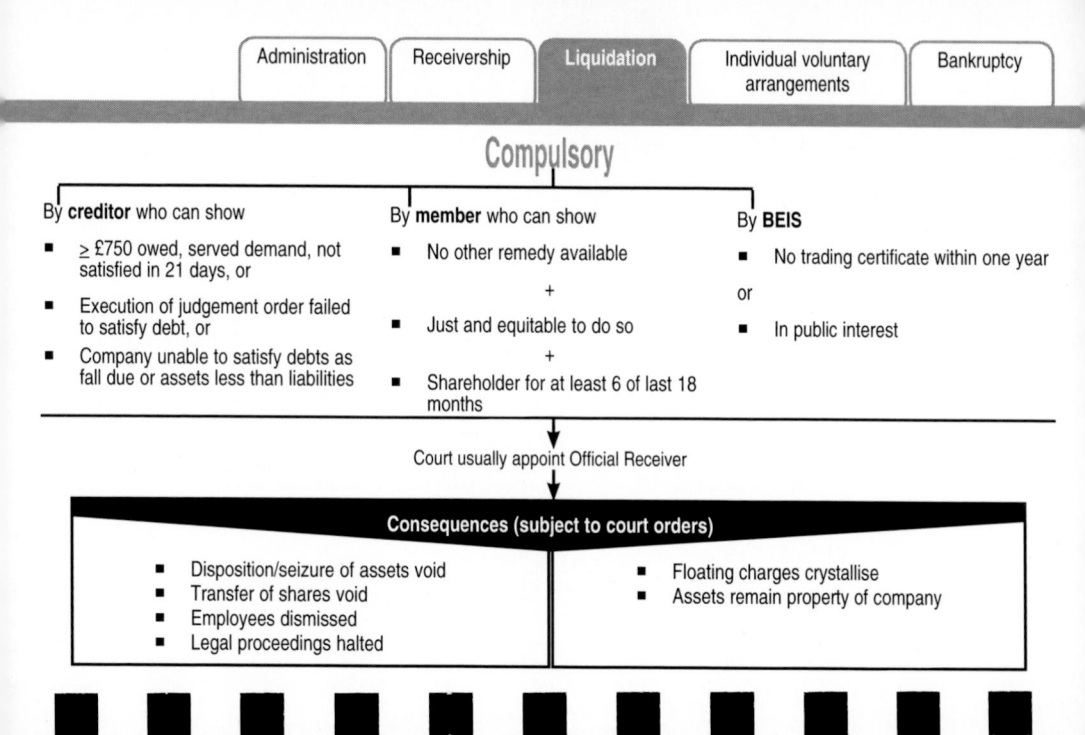

| Administration | Receivership | Liquidation | Individual voluntary arrangements | Bankruptcy |

Compulsory

By creditor who can show

- ≥ £750 owed, served demand, not satisfied in 21 days, or
- Execution of judgement order failed to satisfy debt, or
- Company unable to satisfy debts as fall due or assets less than liabilities

By member who can show

- No other remedy available

    +

- Just and equitable to do so

    +

- Shareholder for at least 6 of last 18 months

By BEIS

- No trading certificate within one year

or

- In public interest

↓

Court usually appoint Official Receiver

↓

Consequences (subject to court orders)

- Disposition/seizure of assets void
- Transfer of shares void
- Employees dismissed
- Legal proceedings halted

- Floating charges crystallise
- Assets remain property of company

Role of liquidator (who assumes directors' powers)

1 Settle list of contributories

2 Collect and realise company's assets

3 Discharge company's debts

4 Distribute surplus to contributories

On completion of liquidation

Voluntary winding up
- Liquidator prepares account of winding up
- Lays it before meeting of members and/or creditors
- Files details with Registrar within one week

Registers details → Company dissolved three months later

Compulsory winding up
- Liquidator goes to court

Court makes order dissolving company

Order filed by liquidator with registrar

Registers details, company dissolved from date of order

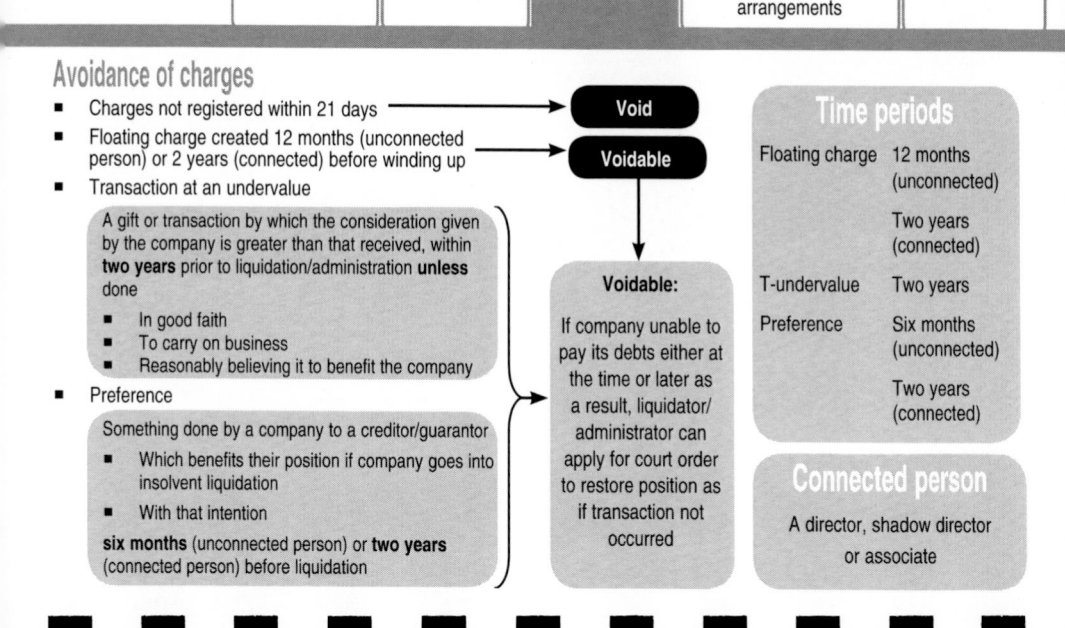

Administration | Receivership | **Liquidation** | Individual voluntary arrangements | Bankruptcy

Avoidance of charges

- Charges not registered within 21 days → **Void**
- Floating charge created 12 months (unconnected person) or 2 years (connected) before winding up → **Voidable**
- Transaction at an undervalue

  A gift or transaction by which the consideration given by the company is greater than that received, within **two years** prior to liquidation/administration **unless** done

  - In good faith
  - To carry on business
  - Reasonably believing it to benefit the company

- Preference

  Something done by a company to a creditor/guarantor

  - Which benefits their position if company goes into insolvent liquidation
  - With that intention

  six months (unconnected person) or **two years** (connected person) before liquidation

Voidable:

If company unable to pay its debts either at the time or later as a result, liquidator/administrator can apply for court order to restore position as if transaction not occurred

Time periods

Floating charge	12 months (unconnected)
	Two years (connected)
T-undervalue	Two years
Preference	Six months (unconnected)
	Two years (connected)

Connected person

A director, shadow director or associate

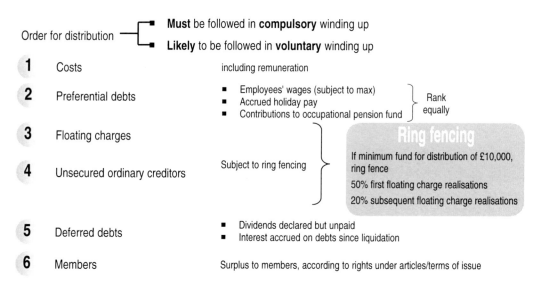

Order for distribution
- **Must** be followed in **compulsory** winding up
- **Likely** to be followed in **voluntary** winding up

1 Costs — including remuneration

2 Preferential debts
- Employees' wages (subject to max)
- Accrued holiday pay
- Contributions to occupational pension fund

} Rank equally

3 Floating charges

4 Unsecured ordinary creditors

Subject to ring fencing

Ring fencing

If minimum fund for distribution of £10,000, ring fence

50% first floating charge realisations

20% subsequent floating charge realisations

5 Deferred debts
- Dividends declared but unpaid
- Interest accrued on debts since liquidation

6 Members — Surplus to members, according to rights under articles/terms of issue

'IVA'

An arrangement by a sole trader/partner/other individual to reach a compromise with their creditors, with the aim of avoiding bankruptcy

Supervised by licensed insolvency practitioners

- Debtor pays reduced amount towards total debt
- Usually over five years
- Approved IVA binds all creditors
- No creditor may petition for bankruptcy (exception if breach of IVA)

Advantages		Disadvantages
☑ No bankruptcy restrictions ☑ Can carry on business		☒ Five years (bankruptcy three years)
☑ Flexibility ☑ Privacy		☒ No opportunity for trustee in bankruptcy to investigate debtor's actions/hidden assets
☑ Cheaper than bankruptcy		

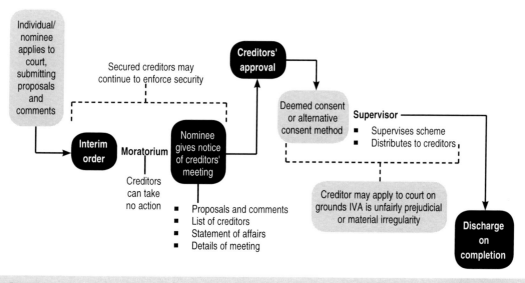

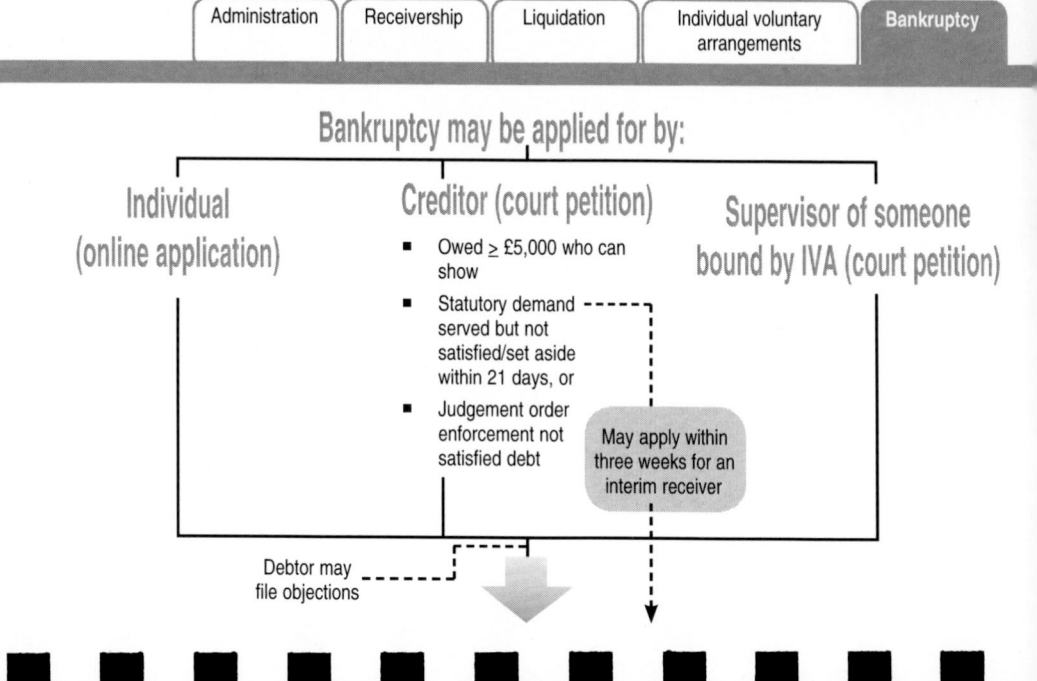

14 days

Court hearing

Bankruptcy order

If satisfied debtor unable to pay debts as fall due

Official receiver/insolvency practitioner appointed as trustee in bankruptcy

- Investigate debtor's financial affairs
- Report to creditors/court
- Notify utilities, local authority, land registry
- Maximise funds
- Pay creditors with provable debts

| Administration | Receivership | Liquidation | Individual voluntary arrangements | Bankruptcy |

Order of distribution

1   Costs   Including remuneration

2   Pre-preferential debts   Eg, funeral expenses

3   Preferential debts
- Employees' wages (subject to max)
- Contribution to occupational pension schemes
- Accrued holiday pay

4   Ordinary debts   Unsecured creditors rank equally
(dividend declared: × pence/£)

5   Interest

6   Postponed debts   Eg, debt to bankrupt's spouse

7   Surplus (rare)   To bankrupt

Consequences of bankruptcy order for 'undischarged bankrupt'

- Estate vests in trustee in bankruptcy
- Trustee manages and protects estate
- Cannot act as director
- Cannot act as insolvency practitioner
- Potential criminal liability for failure to cooperate
- Cannot practice as chartered accountant

Discharge

- One year after order
- Bankruptcy Restrictions Order or Undertaking 2–15 years where culpability

Bankrupt's estate

Excludes
- Items necessary for employment etc
- Items necessary for domestic needs
- Property held on trust for another
- Protected tenancies

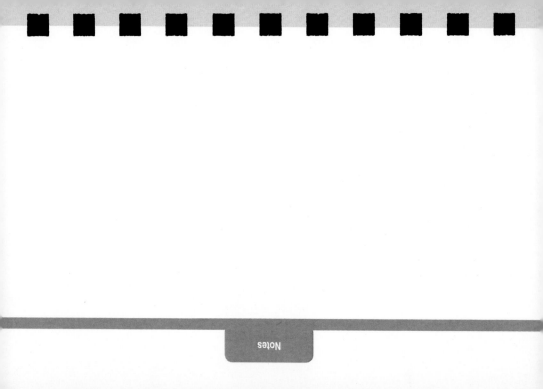

Notes

9: Sole traders and partnerships

Topic List

Sole traders and ordinary partnerships

Comparison between partnerships and companies

Limited liability partnerships

Chapter 9 explains the nature and legal consequences of sole tradership before considering traditional or 'ordinary' partnerships and describing how partnerships differ from a registered company.

The chapter also describes limited liability partnerships registered under the LLP Act 2000.

Sole traders

Sole traders (also known as sole practitioners) own and run businesses which are not legally distinct from the owner. All profits accrue to the owner but they are personally liable for all business debts.

Ordinary partnership ('firm')

The relation which subsists between persons carrying on a business in common with a view of profit

Partnership has no separate legal personality

- Minimum two
- May be individuals or companies

- Can be a single transaction
- Some activity necessary

As 'joint proprietors' (not employer/employee)

Test is one of intention

Note: name

A firm's name can include the word 'company'

Note: formation

No formal agreement is necessary

Fiduciary duties

In addition to duties under the Act and arising out of fiduciary nature of the relationship:

- Act in good faith
- Act for proper motives
- Not retain secret profits
- Avoid conflict of interest

Regulated by **Partnership Act 1890**. In absence of express provision, certain rights, duties and regulatory matters are implied:

Breach may render partner liable to account for monies received and make good losses suffered

Partnership Act provisions (in absence of express agreement to the contrary)

Provision	Partnership Act provision
Profits	Share equally
Losses	Share in same proportions as profits
Management	Every partner can take part in majority decisions
Change in business	Unanimity required
Variation of agreement	Unanimity required
New partners	Unanimity required
Indemnity	Firm indemnifies partners against liabilities ordinarily incurred
Remuneration	No entitlement
Interest on capital	5% only on advances beyond original capital
Records and accounts	■ To be kept in main place of business ■ Open to all partners
Expulsion of partners	■ Majority decision ■ Only if agreement so provides ■ Good faith and good reason
Dissolution	Any partner can require realisation and distribution of assets
Capital deficiency	Shared in proportion to original capital contributions

Liability

Partners are jointly and severally liable for the acts of their fellow partners in so far as they bind the firm, ie, where they have authority

Authority

Each partner is the agent of the firm and their fellow partners for the purpose of the partnership business

Authority may be —
- Express
- Implied
- Ostensible

Restriction on authority

If a partner disregards a restriction placed on their authority, the firm will not be bound **if** the third party has notice of the restriction

P's act is binding on firm and partners **provided** the act is carrying on usual partnership business, and **unless**

(i) They have no authority

and

(ii) The third party either ┬ Knows they have no authority, or
                           └ Does not know or believe them to be a partner

Courts' interpretation

Act should be done

- In the firm's name
- For the purpose of the firm's business
- By a person who purports to act as a partner

Credit

If a partner pledges the firm's credit

- For a purpose that has no apparent connection with the firm's business,
- Without express authority the firm will not be bound

9: Sole traders and partnerships

New partners

Only liable for debts incurred after becoming a partner, unless agrees otherwise

Retiring partners

- Remains liable for pre-retirement debts unless released by creditor
- Liable for post-retirement debts if creditor knew them to be a partner and has not received notice of retirement (hence vital to give notice)

If a partnership defaults on a secured loan, creditor may:

- Sue the firm and/or
- Sue partners individually

If the partnership is insolvent:

- Bankruptcy proceedings may be brought against individual partner(s) and/or
- Partnership may be wound up like an unregistered company

Events causing dissolution

- Death/bankruptcy
- Expiry of fixed term
- Completion of venture
- Illegality
- Notice
- Court order

A partnership agreement usually provides, however, for dissolution only with unanimous consent

Advantages of a company		Advantages of a partnership	
Company	**Partnership**	**Company**	**Partnership**
■ Separate legal entity	■ Not applicable	■ Registration required	■ No formality
■ Members' liability limited	■ Unlimited	■ Need to file accounts and reports etc	■ Not applicable
■ Owns assets	■ Partners own assets	■ Compliance and audit costs	■ Not applicable
■ Continues despite change in membership	■ Dissolution	■ Public inspection rights	■ Not applicable
■ Shares freely transferable	■ Assignee not become partner	■ Members not involved in management (unless also directors)	■ Every partner participates in management
■ Minimum one member	■ Minimum two partners	■ Restrictions on repayment of capital	■ Freedom
■ Can create floating charge	■ Cannot do so		

'LLP'

An incorporated partnership with a separate legal personality.

It is registered like a company and is subject to similar regulation.

Partners (members) are taxed as individuals on partnership profits.

Formation = registration with Registrar of Companies:

Incorporation document:

- Name of LLP -
- Location of registered office (E + W/W)
- Address of registered office
- Members' names and addresses
- Names of designated members
- Fee

Signed by at least two subscribers

Must be on LLP correspondence and outside place of business

Any formal partnership agreement does not need to be filed with the Registrar

- In the absence of express agreement, LLP Act and Regulations apply provisions of companies legislation (to accounts, reports, audit, confirmation statements, etc) and default provisions from Partnership Act 1890 (re profit share, expulsion etc)

  - No maximum number of members

- New members with unanimous agreement

- Membership ceases on giving notice

- Change in membership
  - LLP continues
  - Notify Registrar within 14 days

- Every member participates in management

Unfair prejudice

- Member may apply to court in cases of unfair prejudice (as for a company)
- Right to apply may be excluded for an agreed period with unanimous consent

Liability

The LLP, as a separate legal entity, is liable for the debts and obligations of the business

Exceptionally, an LLP member could face personal liability for professional negligence

Authority

Each member = Agent of LLP

= Binds the LLP by their acts done with authority

An LLP member may be guilty of

- Wrongful trading
- Fraudulent trading

and

- Liable to disqualification

in the same way as a company director

The LLP is NOT bound where

- The member does not have authority

and

- The third party either ⎰ Knows they have no authority, or
  ⎱ Does not know or believe them to be a member of the LLP

Termination of LLP

By unanimous agreement in accordance with LLP agreement (as a second option for termination)

Insolvency options

- Voluntary arrangement
- Administration
- Compulsory liquidation
- Voluntary liquidation

→

- Withdrawals within two years can be claimed back if member knew/had reasonable grounds to believe LLP would become insolvent

- Contribution to assets on a winding up by past and present members will be according to any LLP agreement (position unclear where no express agreement)

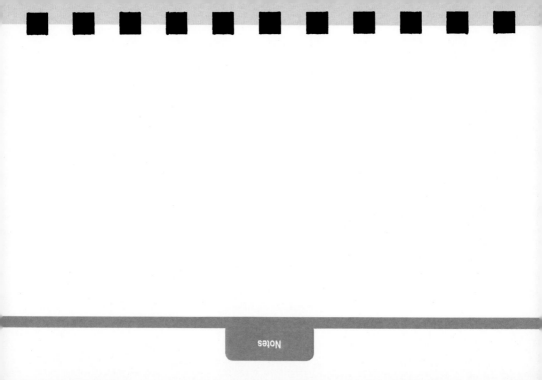

Notes

10: Criminal law

Topic List

Money laundering

Bribery

Fraud

ICAEW Code of Ethics

Whistleblowing

Chapter 10 examines the nature and consequences of various criminal offences, including fraud and fraudulent trading, cyber crime, insider dealing, bribery, corruption and money laundering. It also reviews the ICAEW's Code of Ethics and the statutory protection available to those who 'whistleblow' on their employer.

Money laundering

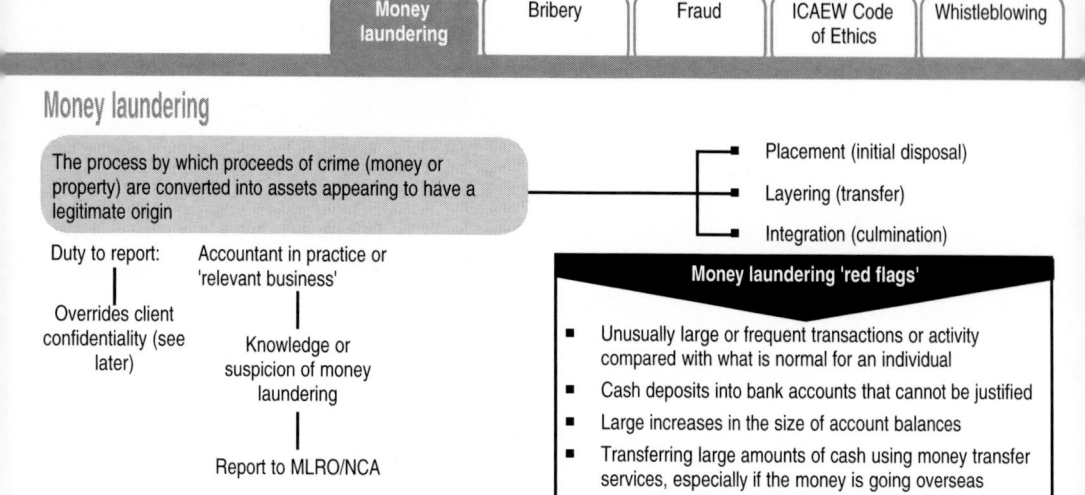

The process by which proceeds of crime (money or property) are converted into assets appearing to have a legitimate origin

- Placement (initial disposal)
- Layering (transfer)
- Integration (culmination)

Duty to report: Accountant in practice or 'relevant business'

Overrides client confidentiality (see later)

Knowledge or suspicion of money laundering

Report to MLRO/NCA

Knowledge

Also not making inquiries

Suspicion

More than speculation

Money laundering 'red flags'

- Unusually large or frequent transactions or activity compared with what is normal for an individual
- Cash deposits into bank accounts that cannot be justified
- Large increases in the size of account balances
- Transferring large amounts of cash using money transfer services, especially if the money is going overseas
- Unwillingness to discuss business activities or provide other business-related information
- Inconsistencies in information being provided (such as different home addresses on ID documentation)

Offences (Proceeds of Crime Act 2002)	Defences	Penalties
1 **Money laundering** ▪ Concealing criminal property ▪ Arranging/being concerned in arrangement ▪ Acquiring/using/possessing ▪ Knowingly inciting/assisting another	▪ Reported to MLRO/NCA ▪ Intended to report but reasonable excuse ▪ Acquired etc for valuable consideration	▪ 14 years ▪ Unlimited fine
2 **Failure to report** ▪ Any knowledge/suspicion that another money laundering ▪ Any information giving reasonable grounds for suspicion (objectively tested)	▪ Reasonable excuse ▪ Legal privilege (see later) ▪ Not know/suspect money laundering and no appropriate training	▪ Five years ▪ Unlimited fine

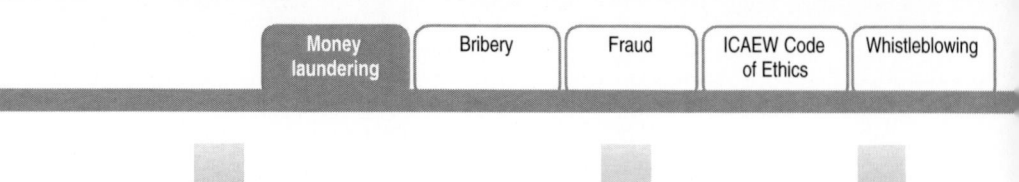

| Money laundering | Bribery | Fraud | ICAEW Code of Ethics | Whistleblowing |

Offences (Proceeds of Crime Act 2002)	Defences	Penalties
3 **Tipping-off** Disclosure of report or investigation where disclosure likely to prejudice investigation	■ Not know/suspect disclosure likely to prejudice investigation ■ Lawful authority or excuse for disclosure	■ Two years ■ Unlimited fine

Confidentiality

- Duty to report overrides client confidentiality
- Statutory protection where lawful report results in breach of confidentiality

Legal professional privilege

- Relevant professional adviser
- Legal advice or litigation
- Defence to failure to report, provided no criminal purpose

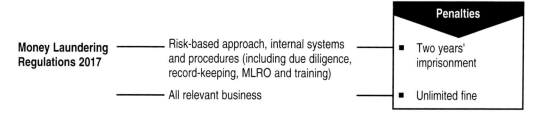

Money Laundering Regulations 2017 —— Risk-based approach, internal systems and procedures (including due diligence, record-keeping, MLRO and training)

—— All relevant business

Penalties

- Two years' imprisonment
- Unlimited fine

Bribery

The **Bribery Act 2010** created four offences concerning Bribery.

Bribing another person

Offering financial or other advantages to induce another to perform a relevant function or activity improperly.

Being bribed

Requesting or accepting financial or other advantages in return for performing a relevant function or activity improperly.

Bribing a foreign public official

Offering financial or other advantages to a foreign official with the intention of influencing that person in their official capacity. A foreign public official is anyone holding a legislative, administrative or judicial position.

Corporate failure to prevent bribery

This is a corporate offence which is commited by an organisation that fails to prevent a bribery offence being commited by anyone that represents the organisation. An organisation has a defence if it has 'adequate procedures' in place to prevent bribery.

Fraud Act 2006

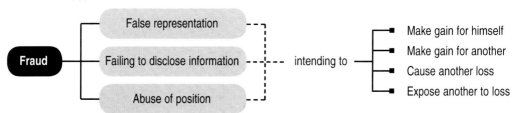

Fraud

- False representation
- Failing to disclose information
- Abuse of position

--- intending to ---

- Make gain for himself
- Make gain for another
- Cause another loss
- Expose another to loss

Penalties

- 10 years' imprisonment
- unlimited fine

Fraud and cyber crime

National Crime Agency (NCA)

Cyber threats

- Phishing
- Webcam manager
- File hijacker
- Keylogging
- Screenshot manager
- Ad clicker

Types of cyber-enabled fraud

- Electronic financial fraud
- Fraudulent sales through online auction or retail sites
- Mass-marketing frauds and consumer scams
- Phishing scams
- Pharming
- 'Online romance' (or social networking/dating website) fraud

Cyber crime protection

- Firewalls
- Secure configurations
- Access controls
- Virus and malware protection
- Patch management

The Computer Misuse Act 1990

Aims to secure computer material against unauthorised access or modification; and for connected purposes.

It makes the following illegal:

- Unauthorised access to computer material

- Unauthorised access with intent to commit or facilitate commission of further offences

- Unauthorised acts with intent to impair, or with recklessness as to impairing, operation of computer, etc

- Unauthorised acts causing, or creating risk of, serious damage

- Making, supplying or obtaining articles for use in the above offences

Fraudulent trading

Occurs where a business is carried on with intent to defraud creditors or for any fraudulent purpose

- Whether or not company in liquidation
- Can also be committed by non-corporate trader

By any person 'knowingly a party' to fraudulent trading — Subjective
- Some positive act
- Some dishonesty

Penalties

1 Unlimited fine

2 10 years' imprisonment

3 Disqualification (discretionary: 2–15 years)

Alert! Also civil offence: in liquidation only, resulting in liability for company's debts

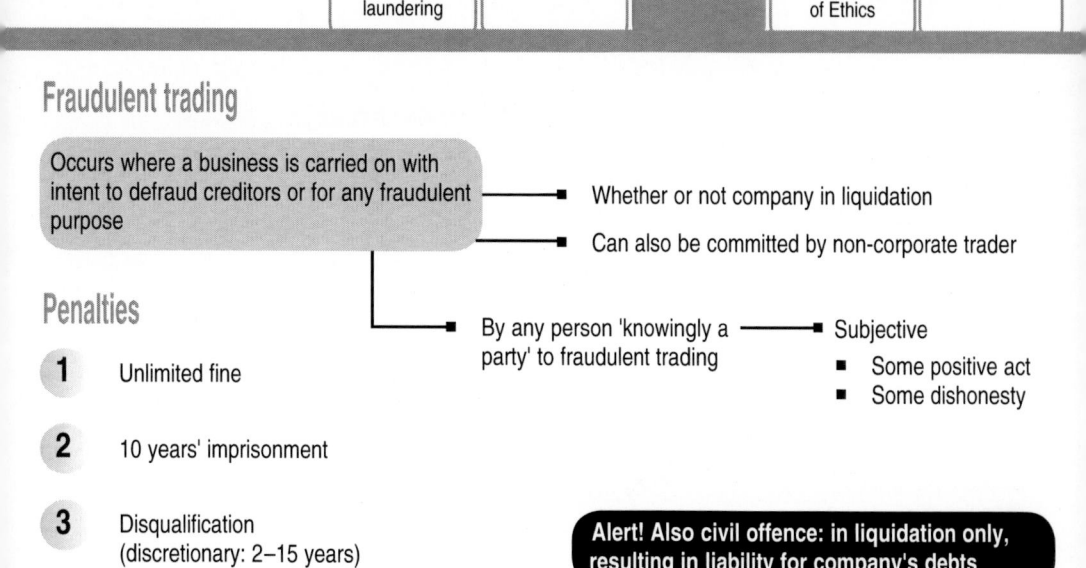

Insider dealing

1 Insider dealing

Dealing in securities while possessing price-sensitive **insider information** as **insider**

— Any dealing

— Directly/through agent

— Irrelevant whether
- Person knows securities price-affected
- Inside information given
- Dealing takes place

2 Encourage another to deal

Reasonably believing dealing will take place

3 Disclosing information

Other than in proper performance of employment, office or profession

Inside information

Specific information, not made public, relating to a particular issuer of securities – would have significant effect on price if made public

Insider

(a) Director, employee or shareholder

or

(b) Access due to employment or office

or

(c) Through either source

Defences

- Not expect profit
- Believed disclosed widely
- Would have anyway

Penalties

- Unlimited fine
- Seven years' imprisonment

ICAEW Code of Ethics

Fundamental Principles

Integrity: straightforward and honest in business and professional relationships.

Objectivity: not allow bias, conflict of interest or influence of others to override professional or business judgement.

Professional competence and due care: be aware of all prevailing knowledge necessary to give professional service and apply the same diligently to affairs of the client in accordance with technical and professional standards.

Confidentiality: respect the confidentiality of information acquired as a consequence of professional or business engagements and not use the same for personal advantage or that of third parties.

Professional behaviour: comply with laws and regulations and not to discredit the profession.

Threats and safeguards

The Code identifies a number of threats to these ethical principles and sets out safeguards that an accountant can use to protect themselves. There are separate threats and safeguards of accountants in business and in public practice.

Whistleblowing

describes where a **worker** discloses a wrongdoing, usually by their employer

Public Interest Disclosure Act 1998

- Statutory protection from any 'detriment'
- 'Automatically unfair' dismissal if employee
- Unlimited compensation
- No minimum age/length of service

Qualifying disclosure

Worker's **reasonable belief** shows

1 Criminal offence
2 Failure of legal obligation
3 Miscarriage of justice
4 Danger to health and safety
5 Danger to environment
6 Cover up

Public interest

- Not defined
- Compensation may be reduced by up to 25% if not made in good faith

To appropriate person

1 Internal
2 In course of legal advice
3 Minister of Crown
4 Prescribed regulator eg, HSE, HMRC, FCA
5 Wider
  - Reasonable in circumstances
  - Not personal gain
  - Reasonable belief victimised/cover up or already raised

Notes

11: Employment, data protection and intellectual property law

Chapter 11 examines the concept of employee status: how it is established and identified and the significance of the distinction between employees and independent contractors. It then explains the rights of employees to seek redress in the case of unfair dismissal, wrongful dismissal and redundancy.

This chapter also describes the principal provisions of the Data Protection Act, before concluding with material on intellectual property.

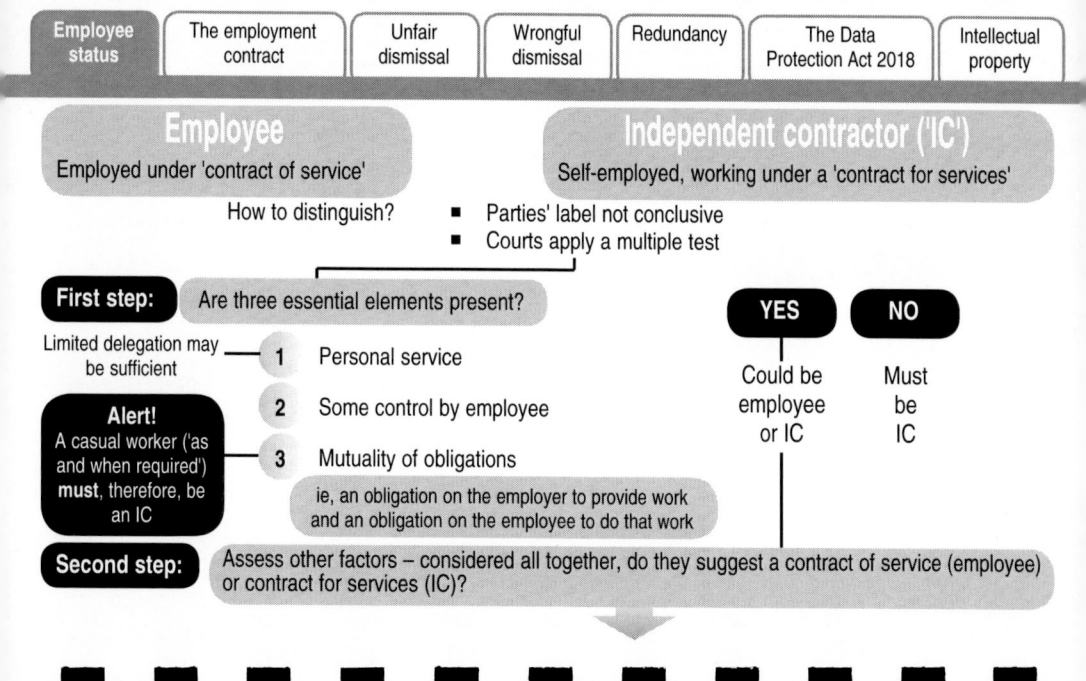

Employee
Employed under 'contract of service'

Independent contractor ('IC')
Self-employed, working under a 'contract for services'

How to distinguish?
- Parties' label not conclusive
- Courts apply a multiple test

First step: Are three essential elements present?

YES — Could be employee or IC

NO — Must be IC

Limited delegation may be sufficient

1 Personal service

2 Some control by employee

Alert!
A casual worker ('as and when required') **must**, therefore, be an IC

3 Mutuality of obligations

ie, an obligation on the employer to provide work and an obligation on the employee to do that work

Second step: Assess other factors – considered all together, do they suggest a contract of service (employee) or contract for services (IC)?

Other factors applied in multiple test:

> **Remember!**
> - Total freedom to delegate will mean IC status
> - Limited power (eg in the event of illness or to restricted persons) may be consistent with employee status
> - Total prohibition will indicate employee status more strongly

	More consistent with employee status	More consistent with IC status
Can they delegate?	No	Yes
Does employer exercise control? (eg, over what, how, when, for how long, where?	Yes	No
Is there a mutuality of obligations?	Yes	No
Is there provision for holiday and/or sick pay?	Yes	No
Does the employer provide the tools and equipment?	Yes	No
Does the worker wear a uniform or display the employer's logo?	Yes	No
Can they utilise the employer's support staff?	Yes	No
Is tax/NI deducted at source?	Yes	No
Do they assume responsibility for investment/risk?	No	Yes
Do they work for more than one person?	No	Yes
How long has the working relationship existed?	Longer	Shorter

Other considerations

- All contractual terms
- The nature of the claim

> **Remember!**
> - If none exists, they must be IC
> - If present, it counts as evidence of employee status

11: Employment, data protection and intellectual property law

The practical significance of the distinction between an employee and an IC

	Employee	IC
Can they claim for wrongful dismissal?	✓	✗

Do they benefit from employment protection?

	Employee	IC
■ Minimum periods of notice	✓	✗
■ Statutory redundancy payments	✓	✗
■ Remedies for unfair dismissal	✓	✗
■ Health and safety	✓	(✗)

Note: Many health and safety obligations benefit ICs (and others) also. Increasingly, employment protection is given to 'workers', a term more widely defined than 'employees', eg, working time protection

	Employee	IC
Do they have preferential rights as a creditor in the event of the employer's insolvency?	✓	✗
Are duties and rights implied into the contract?	✓	✗

Note: An IC is directly responsible to HMRC (schedule D)

	Employee	IC
Is the employer vicariously liable for their tortious acts?	✓	✗
Must income tax be deducted at source?	✓	✗

Note: There are also differences in statutory sick pay amounts and levies for industrial training purposes

	Employee	IC
Might they need to register for, and charge, VAT?	✗	✓
How are social security contributions made?	Class 1	Class 2 + 4

Contract

Oral or written

Terms implied by law

- A statement of prescribed particulars must be given within **two months** if there is no contract covering them.

- The statement may provide **evidence** of any contract between the parties.

In event of breach:

- Employee can apply for declaration

- Compensation may be available in unfair dismissal claim

No contract

Prescribed particulars

- Names of employer and employee
- Date employment began
- Whether previous employment included in continuous service
- Pay: when and how much
- Hours of work
- Job title
- Holiday/holiday pay entitlement
- Sick leave/sick pay entitlement
- Pension
- Length of termination notice
- Disciplinary procedures

May be given in separate documents

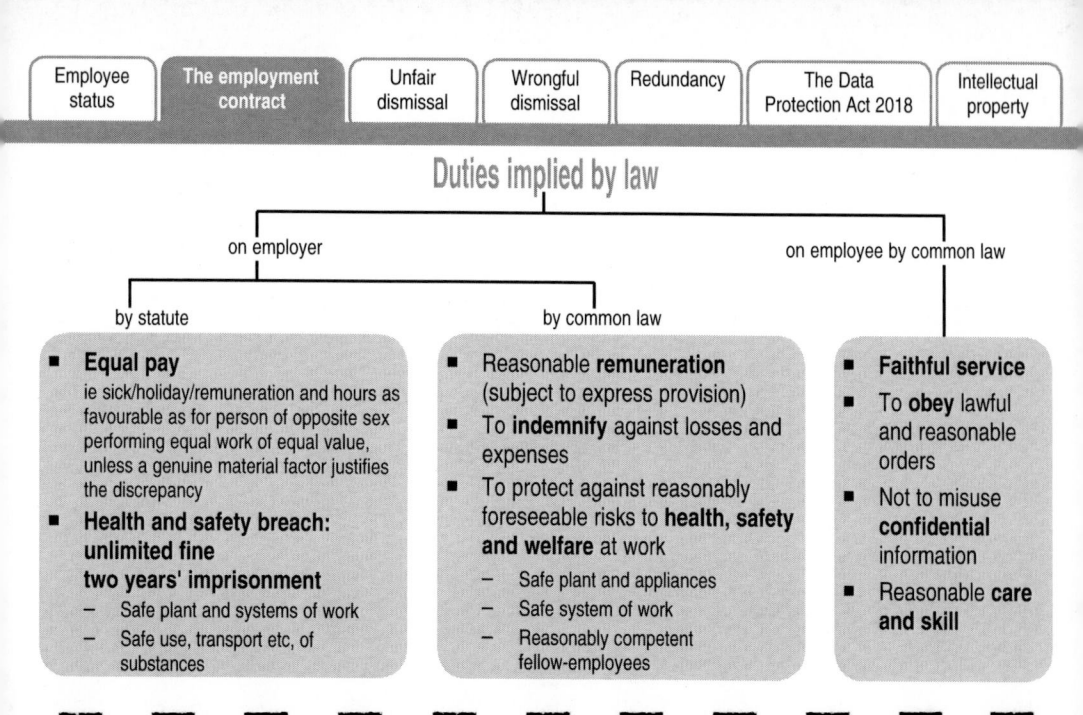

Duties implied by law

on employer

by statute

- **Equal pay**
  ie sick/holiday/remuneration and hours as favourable as for person of opposite sex performing equal work of equal value, unless a genuine material factor justifies the discrepancy
- **Health and safety breach: unlimited fine two years' imprisonment**
  - Safe plant and systems of work
  - Safe use, transport etc, of substances

by common law

- Reasonable **remuneration** (subject to express provision)
- To **indemnify** against losses and expenses
- To protect against reasonably foreseeable risks to **health, safety and welfare** at work
  - Safe plant and appliances
  - Safe system of work
  - Reasonably competent fellow-employees

on employee by common law

- **Faithful service**
- To **obey** lawful and reasonable orders
- Not to misuse **confidential** information
- Reasonable **care and skill**

- – Adequate information, training, supervision
- – Safe work place and access
- – Safe and healthy working environment
- **Discrimination**
  (race, sex, disability, religion, age, sexual orientation)
- **Minimum period of notice**

- To provide **work** (or to continue to pay wages)
- To be fair and accurate in any **reference**
- Not to disclose **confidential** information
- **Trust and confidence**
- Reasonable **notice**

- **Personal service** (ie, not to delegate without employer's express/implied consent)
- **Trust and confidence**

So liability is more likely where employee is on commission

Alert!
There is no obligation to provide a reference, but if they do, the employer must ensure it is fair and accurate and does not disclose facts not known to the employee

Minimum period of notice

Continuous employment	Minimum notice
1 month – 2 years	1 week
2 years – 12 years	1 week per year
12 years plus	12 weeks

- Entitlement to notice may be **waived** or a sum paid in lieu (if agreed)

- During the period of notice, employee entitled to **pay** $\geq$ average earnings over the past 12 weeks

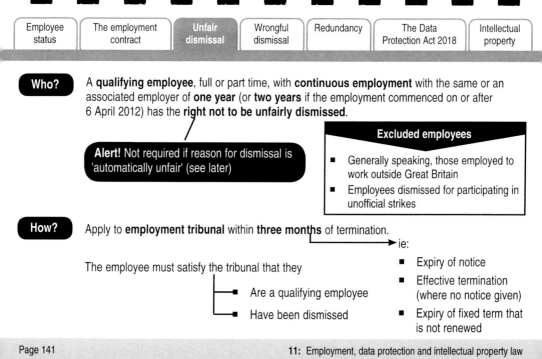

Who?

A **qualifying employee**, full or part time, with **continuous employment** with the same or an associated employer of **one year** (or **two years** if the employment commenced on or after 6 April 2012) has the **right not to be unfairly dismissed**.

Alert! Not required if reason for dismissal is 'automatically unfair' (see later)

Excluded employees

- Generally speaking, those employed to work outside Great Britain
- Employees dismissed for participating in unofficial strikes

How?

Apply to **employment tribunal** within **three months** of termination.

The employee must satisfy the tribunal that they

- Are a qualifying employee
- Have been dismissed

ie:

- Expiry of notice
- Effective termination (where no notice given)
- Expiry of fixed term that is not renewed

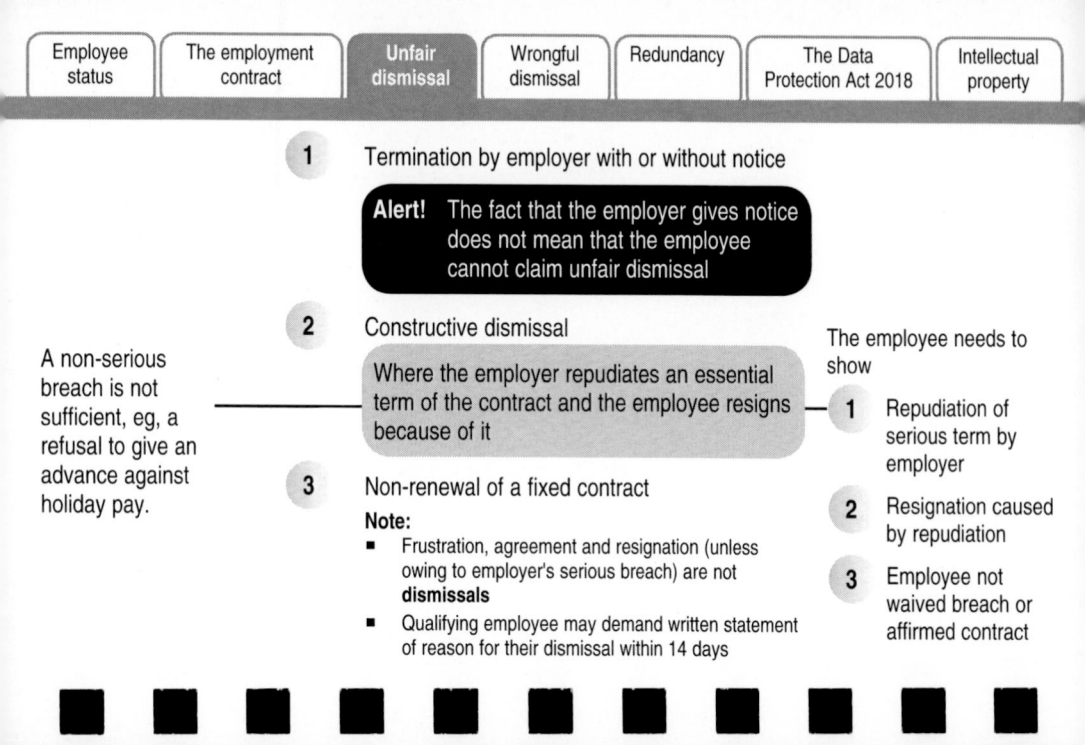

1 Termination by employer with or without notice

> **Alert!** The fact that the employer gives notice does not mean that the employee cannot claim unfair dismissal

2 Constructive dismissal

A non-serious breach is not sufficient, eg, a refusal to give an advance against holiday pay.

Where the employer repudiates an essential term of the contract and the employee resigns because of it

3 Non-renewal of a fixed contract

Note:
- Frustration, agreement and resignation (unless owing to employer's serious breach) are not **dismissals**
- Qualifying employee may demand written statement of reason for their dismissal within 14 days

The employee needs to show

1 Repudiation of serious term by employer

2 Resignation caused by repudiation

3 Employee not waived breach or affirmed contract

The dismissal may be either 'automatically unfair' or 'potentially fair'

Automatically unfair reasons

- **Pregnancy**/pregnancy-related illness
- Spent **conviction**
- **TU** membership/activities
- **Transfer** of undertaking (unless justifying reasons)
- Taking steps to avert imminent danger
- Seeking to enforce **statutory rights**
- Making a **protected disclosure**

↓

Remember!

There is no requirement for the employee to have one year's continuous employment in these cases

Potentially fair reasons

1   Lack of capability or qualifications
- Objectively and subjectively assessed
- Employer to show that it is sufficiently serious
- May arise from one or more incidents
- There must be a contractual obligation to hold the qualification

2   Misconduct
- Genuine and reasonable belief on employer's part is sufficient

3   Redundancy
- Employee must show other employees were alternative choices for redundancy and that selection was in breach of customary agreed procedure or because of TU membership

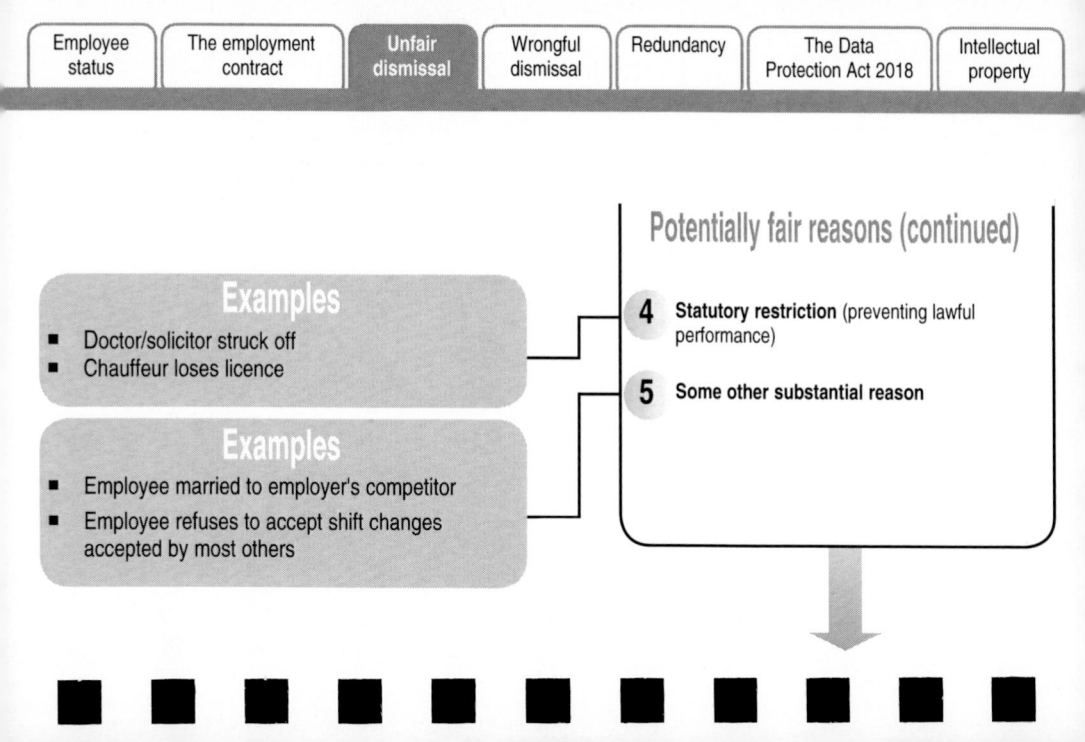

Procedure where dismissal is **not** for **automatically unfair** reason:

Employee shows dismissed → Employer shows principal reason for dismissal **and** that it was 'potentially fair' → If tribunal satisfied → Tribunal considers whether employer acted reasonably → If satisfied → **Dismissal fair**

If not satisfied → **Dismissal unfair**

Employer shows principal reason for dismissal **and** that it was 'potentially fair' → If tribunal not satisfied → **Dismissal unfair**

Remember!

Award may be increased or decreased by up to 25% on account of breach of disciplinary/grievance procedures in Acas Code

Employer's reasonableness is a **question of fact**, depending on circumstances:

- Procedures followed (including Acas Code)?
- Advice, training or supervision offered?
- What would a reasonable employer have done?
- Warning given?
- Consultation had?
- Alternatives considered? (eg, demotion)
- Fairness to employer's business needs

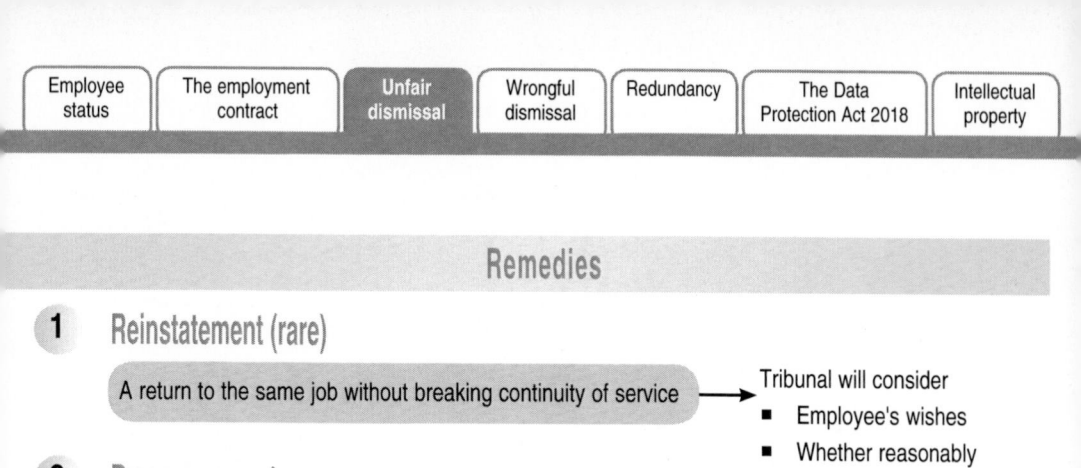

Remedies

1 Reinstatement (rare)

A return to the same job without breaking continuity of service → Tribunal will consider
- Employee's wishes
- Whether reasonably practicable

2 Re-engagement

Suitable alternative employment on comparable terms → Will not be ordered where confidence has broken down between the parties

3

Compensation

3a Basic award

Calculated by reference to age and length of service (subject to statutory maximum)

3b Compensatory award

Such amount as is just and equitable in all the circumstances, taking into account the employer's actions and the basic award

3c Additional award

Between 26 and 52 weeks' pay

→ The **basic** award may be **reduced**

- By amount of redundancy payment
- If offer of reinstatement unreasonably refused
- If just and equitable on the basis of employee's conduct

→ The **compensatory** award may be **reduced**

- Where the employee fails to mitigate their loss
- Where employee's conduct caused or contributed to the dismissal

→ The **additional** award will only be ordered where the employer fails to comply with reinstatement/re-engagement order and does not show that it was impracticable to do so

Wrongful dismissal

A common law action taken by an employee who has been dismissed by their employer in breach of contract

Wrongful dismissal occurs where there is a dismissal:

1 With **no notice**

2 With **insufficient notice**

3 **Before the expiry** of a fixed term/specified task contract

4 For **redundancy** in breach of an agreed selection procedure

5 By the employer's **repudiation** of the contract, 'accepted' by the employee's consequent **resignation**

6 For a **reason outside specific reasons** given in the contract

Remedies

Damages

- Based on loss of earnings
- Usually earnings attributable to notice period (plus actual/potential benefits to which entitled)
- Duty to mitigate
- Conduct of parties irrelevant

Injunction (rare)

- To restrain a breach of contract

Declaration

- As to the employee's rights

equitable remedies in the court's discretion

If the contract provides for the payment of a **sum in lieu of notice**, the employee may sue for it under the contract

This is **not** wrongful dismissal

The employee is under no duty to mitigate their loss

Which court?

- Usually County Court/High Court
- Employment tribunals also have jurisdiction

Why wrongful dismissal instead of unfair dismissal?

- Damages could be higher.. statutory maximum in unfair dismissal

- Unfair dismissal might be time-barred...................... unfair dismissal must be brought within three months

- Dismissal might be 'fair' but still 'wrongful'................. eg, where insufficient notice is given

- Employee might not 'qualify' for unfair dismissal......... eg, might not have one year's continuous employment

Summary dismissal

A justified dismissal without proper notice

Question of fact

Based on objective standards prevailing at the time

Examples

1. Wilful refusal to obey a lawful and reasonable order
2. Gross misconduct eg, secret commissions/assault on fellow employee
3. Dishonesty/breach of trust
4. Gross or persistent negligence
5. Breach of contract term/rules where zero tolerance clear
6. Continuation not possible eg, employer dies/partnership dissolved/company wound up

Remember!

Usually in connection with the business, but also outside, if sufficiently grave

| Employee status | The employment contract | Unfair dismissal | Wrongful dismissal | **Redundancy** | The Data Protection Act 2018 | Intellectual property |

Redundancy

A dismissal where the only or main reason is

- The employer has ceased, or intends to cease, to carry on **the business** in which the employee has worked

- The employer has ceased, or intends to cease, to carry out the business in **the place** in which the employee has worked

- The requirements of that business for employees to carry on work of a **particular kind**, or at a particular place have ceased or diminished

A question of fact

Mobility clause

- Dismissal in accordance with an express mobility clause is not redundancy

- A mobility clause must be fair and reasonable, in accordance with the implied duty of trust and confidence

- 'The place where the employee was employed' (in deciding whether redundancy occurred) does not include every place where they **could** have worked under a mobility clause

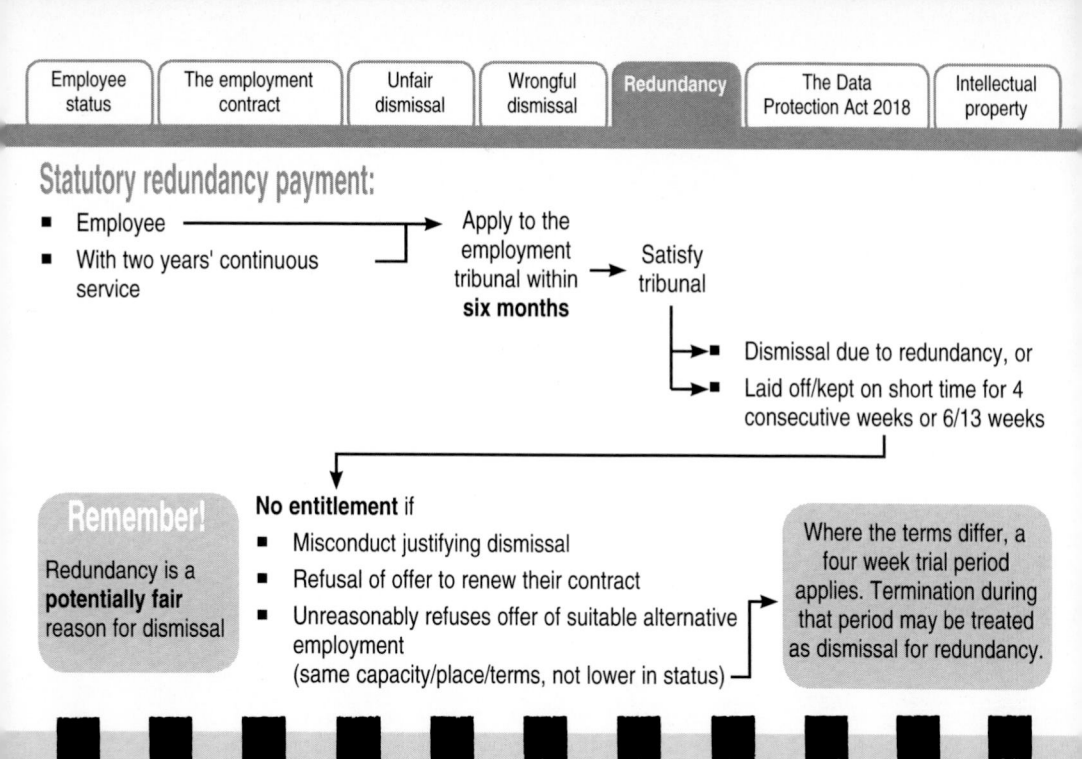

Statutory redundancy payment:

- Employee
- With two years' continuous service

→ Apply to the employment tribunal within **six months** → Satisfy tribunal

- Dismissal due to redundancy, or
- Laid off/kept on short time for 4 consecutive weeks or 6/13 weeks

No entitlement if

- Misconduct justifying dismissal
- Refusal of offer to renew their contract
- Unreasonably refuses offer of suitable alternative employment (same capacity/place/terms, not lower in status)

Remember!

Redundancy is a **potentially fair** reason for dismissal

Where the terms differ, a four week trial period applies. Termination during that period may be treated as dismissal for redundancy.

| Employee status | The employment contract | Unfair dismissal | Wrongful dismissal | Redundancy | **The Data Protection Act 2018** | Intellectual property |

Data controller

Determines the purpose and means of processing personal data.

Data processor

Responsible for the processing of personal data on behalf of a controller.

Data subject

Identified or identifiable individuals (not companies) to whom personal data relates.

DPA (enacts the EU's General Data Protection Regulation – GDPR)

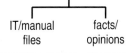

IT/manual files   facts/opinions

Enforcement

- The Information Commissioner has the power to act where there is non-compliance
- The IC must be notified within 72 hours of a data breach affecting individuals' rights and freedoms
- Fine of up to £17 million or 4% of global turnover
- Criminal conviction where a criminal offence occurs

GDPR data protection principles

1 Lawfulness, fairness and transparency

2 Purpose limitation

3 Data minimisation

4 Accuracy

5 Storage limitation

6 Integrity and confidentiality (security)

Rights under GDPR

- Right to be informed
- Right of access
- Right to rectification
- Right to erasure
- Right to restrict processing
- Right to data portability
- Right to object
- Rights in relation to automated decision making and profiling

| Employee status | The employment contract | Unfair dismissal | Wrongful dismissal | Redundancy | The Data Protection Act 2018 | Intellectual property |

Intellectual property

Intellectual property (IP) is a form of intangible asset that a company creates through the application of the skill and knowledge of its employees

Examples of IP	Methods of IP protection
■ The names of products or brands ■ Inventions ■ The design or look of products ■ Items that the company wrote, made or produced	■ Copyright ■ Design right ■ Trademark ■ Registered design ■ Patent

IP legislation and offences

Trade Mark Act 1994 Unauthorised use of a trade mark	A gain is made, or a loss is created through the unauthorised use of a trademark. For example a website uses the trademark of another business in order to gain sales or deprive the real owner of sales.
Copyright, Designs and Patent Act 1988 Criminal liability for making, dealing with or using illicit recordings	Selling, hiring or exhibiting copyrighted material. For example, the public performance of copyrighted music, such as a business streaming music to its customers.
Registered Designs Act 1949 Offence of unauthorised copying etc. of design in course of business	Creating a product using the exact or materially similar design specifications of another product.
Fraud Act 2006 Fraud by false representation	Making a gain or causing a loss by making a fraudulent representation about a product. For example, passing off a product as made by one company when in fact it is a copy.